FOR THE LAST DAYS

Living All Out for Jesus in the Judgement Hour of Earth's History

FOR THE LAST DAYS

Living All Out for Jesus in the Judgement Hour of Earth's History

RANDY MAXWELL

Pacific Press® Publishing Association

Nampa, Idaho | Oshawa, Ontario, Canada
www.pacificpress.com

Cover design by Gerald Lee Monks
Cover design resources from iStockphoto.com
Inside design by Aaron Troia

Copyright © 2016 by Pacific Press® Publishing Association
Printed in the United States of America
All rights reserved

The author assumes full responsibility for the accuracy of all facts and quotations as cited in this book.

Unless otherwise noted, Scripture quotations are from the HOLY BIBLE, NEW INTERNATIONAL VERSION®. Copyright © 1973, 1978, 1984, 2011 by Biblica, Inc®.Used by permission. All rights reserved worldwide.

Scripture quotations marked AMP are taken from the Amplified Bible, copyright © 1954, 1958, 1962, 1964, 1965, 1987 by the Lockman Foundation. Used by permission.

Scripture quotations marked HCSB are taken from the Holman Christian Standard Bible®, copyright © 1999, 2000, 2002, 2003 by Holman Bible Publishers. Used by permission. Holman Christian Standard Bible®, Holman CSB®, and HCSB® are federally registered trademarks of Holman Bible Publishers.

Scripture quotations marked KJV are from the King James Version.

Scripture quotations marked *The Message* are taken from *The Message*. Copyright © 1993, 1994, 1995, 1996, 2000, 2001, 2002. Used by permission of NavPress Publishing Group.

Scripture quotations marked NASB are taken from the NEW AMERICAN STANDARD BIBLE®, copyright © 1960, 1962, 1963, 1968, 1971, 1972, 1973, 1975, 1977, 1995 by the Lockman Foundation. Used by permission.

Scripture quotations marked NKJV are taken from the New King James Version®. Copyright © 1982 by Thomas Nelson, Inc. Used by permission. All rights reserved.

Scripture quotations marked NLT are taken from the *Holy Bible*, New Living Translation, copyright © 1996, 2004, 2015 by Tyndale House Foundation. Used by permission of Tyndale House Publishers, Inc., Carol Stream, Illinois 60188. All rights reserved.

Additional copies of this book are available by calling toll-free 1-800-765-6955 or by visiting www.AdventistBookCenter.com.

Library of Congress Cataloging-in-Publication Data
Names: Maxwell, Randy, author.
Title: Boot camp for the last days : living all out for Jesus in the judgement hour of earth's history / Randy Maxwell.
Description: Nampa : Pacific Press Publishing, 2016.
Identifiers: LCCN 2016029015 | ISBN 9780816361939 (pbk.)
Subjects: LCSH: Christian life. | Second Advent. | General Conference of Seventh-day Adventists—Doctrines.
Classification: LCC BV4509.5 .M34153 2016 | DDC 248.4/867—dc23 LC record available at https://lccn.loc.gov/2016029015

September 2016

Dedication

To the Kuna, Idaho, Seventh-day Adventist Church family who took a chance on this rookie pastor and allowed Suzette and me to serve you for ten years. Thank you. Stay ready.

And to my aunt, Barbara Barker, who passed to her rest while this book was in the final stages of publication. She excelled in God's boot camp. I can't wait to see this mother-in-Israel and prayer warrior receive Christ's "medal of honor" on "Graduation Day."

Acknowledgments

Jason Whitson: Without your encouragement (make that insistence!), this book may never have made it to publication. Thanks for the push.

Amanda Withers: I'm glad my seventh book turned out to be among your first assignments as a new editor. (The same position God called me to thirty years ago! Isn't serving God a hoot?) You wear it well. Thank you!

Contents

Introduction 9

1. Fit for Heaven 11

2. Defensive Dining 21

3. The Last Message 31

4. Worthy Worship 41

5. Don't Drink the Kool-Aid 50

6. The "March" of the Beast 58

7. Endurance Training 72

8. Jesus Rising 81

Epilogue: Now! 89

Introduction

About three hours before I sat down to type this introduction, I received a text message from a friend whose child serves in the United States (US) military. Her text had an edge of anxiety as she related the news that her child's base was going on lockdown due to an imminent attack. No one was being allowed off base. The enemy (yes, I'm being intentionally vague) was stockpiling weapons for a full-scale attack against the base.

I immediately petitioned the God of heaven to provide a shield of protection around this soldier whom I had the privilege of pastoring and watching grow up. I prayed that the plans of the enemy would fail and that no harm would come to the young man or his fellow soldiers on the base. All of his training is now going to come into play in a real life-and-death situation.

The imminent threat my young parishioner faces is but a microcosm of the imminent threat our nation and our world face from a cosmic enemy. "We do not wrestle against flesh and blood, but against principalities, against powers, against the rulers of the darkness of this age, against spiritual hosts of wickedness in the heavenly places" (Ephesians 6:12, NKJV).

At this writing, not a week passes without a major act of terror abroad and at home. Our flags fly at half-mast so often now that it is becoming the default position. Unprovoked shootings of citizens at the hands of law-enforcement officers and retaliatory ambushes on those officers have horrified us and set the nation on edge. The fear of foreign terrorist organizations wreaking havoc on American soil may be misplaced as American citizens wage war on each other with rhetoric and weapons.

> Justice is turned back,
> And righteousness stands afar off;
> For truth is fallen in the street,
> And equity cannot enter (Isaiah 59:14, NKJV).

Boot Camp for the Last Days

What is happening in literally every part of the globe is not a test. It is an actual emergency, and this book is about being spiritually prepared for what is to come. It is "basic training" for the last days, and as everyone knows, basic training takes place in boot camp. Welcome to camp!

Boot camp transforms a civilian into a soldier. It's a time of focus, intensity, and discipline, and a time of learning survival skills. As my young friend is finding out even now, his training was real because the war is real. Our training, too, must be real because the war we're in—seen and unseen—is just as real.

So what "basic training" do we need? The Word of God for sure and, more specifically, the messages of the three angels in Revelation 14. These special messages—the final ones given to the earth's inhabitants before Jesus returns—contain both the instructions and the training necessary to meet the coming crisis.

Although the fourteenth chapter of the Apocalypse may be familiar territory to you, please don't assume a nothing-new-here attitude. Wait. I want you to revisit these messages through the lens of a Christlike character. This is not another prophecy *information* boot camp. It's a prophecy *transformation* boot camp. Character is what it's all about and if we miss that, we are vulnerable to attack. It does us absolutely no good to know the identity of the beast and not know Jesus.

Rather than a lockdown, it's time for us to lock in—lock in on the true and everlasting gospel; lock in on unprecedented and prevailing prayer; lock in on worthy worship; lock in on true Sabbath rest; lock in on the Word, and lock out compromise; lock in on a real relationship with God that allows Jesus to rise in all we do and say.

This is the bottom line to this book: if Jesus isn't rising in my life, if He isn't my heart's desire and obsession, I may miss the main purpose of prophecy—to prepare me to be with the One I love. We're not just preparing for war, we're preparing for a wedding. Are you ready?

As I do for my young friend who is in harm's way, I pray to the God of heaven for a shield of protection about us as we enter His boot camp. I pray that the plans of the enemy will fail and that nothing will stop us from the character transformation we need to get *ready for the wedding and serious about the war.*

1

Fit for Heaven

Therefore, with minds that are alert and fully sober, set your hope on the grace to be brought to you when Jesus Christ is revealed at his coming.
—1 Peter 1:13

Jesus is coming soon! Oh, stop it! If He didn't come at the end of 2015, when will He ever come? For many, the conditions couldn't have been more right. September 2015 was an apocalyptic perfect storm. A Jesuit pope came to America and addressed the US Congress—a first for any pope. The fourth "blood moon" occurred on September 27. The Shemitah [sabbatical] year expired. The rapture was to occur during Rosh Hashanah, and the world was to end at the hands of CERN—a nuclear research facility in Switzerland experimenting with separating the so-called God particle. Some predicted Earth would be vaporized on September 23.

But the perfect apocalyptic storm passed, and doubters lifted their glasses to toast their survival at yet another end-of-the-world party. Let's get real. Most people didn't even know about all those end-time overtones. It was just another month. Jesus coming soon? Yeah, right.

There were doubters about Jesus' first coming; there were doubters about His resurrection, and there are doubters today about His second coming. Nothing new there. But if we count ourselves among those who believe that He *is* coming back, how does that belief impact our lives? This is an all-important question, meriting further study and discussion.

Why is it important to process what it means to be ready for Christ's coming and how it affects our everyday lives? Because many are losing faith at the time we need it most. This book will take us on a soul search—one that lands us in God's boot camp for the last days.

Boot Camp for the Last Days

When you hear the words *boot camp,* you probably think of discipline, rigorous training, and hard work—and you'd be right. What makes boot camps different? The difference is in focus and intensity. I own a *Biggest Loser* DVD workout program that contains three different workouts—cardiovascular, strength training, and Boot Camp. As I began researching boot camps, I decided to try out this Boot Camp workout. I immediately noticed a difference—it was faster paced, with fewer breaks and increased intensity!

Out-of-the-ordinary training takes place to produce an out-of-the-ordinary result. *Boot camp is getting serious about anything you take seriously.* There's no boot camp for couch surfing. And there's no boot camp for pew warming, either!

In the military, boot camp is also known as basic training. From many questions and comments I've heard, it is evident that we could use some basic training on what we believe and why—how to *diligently* seek Him during the days of waiting just prior to Christ's return.

I asked a member of my congregation named Brian (an Iraq War veteran) about his experience in boot camp. He confirmed the transformational aspect of boot camp by telling me that it turns you from an individual into something the army deems trainable. He said their goal is to tear down all the independent thinking, which lines up exactly with something I read online: "The training programs are scientifically and psychologically designed to tear apart the 'civilian' and build from scratch a proud, physically fit, and dedicated member of the United States Armed Forces."[1]

You learn how to be a grown-up. You learn discipline. You're given a uniform and a haircut, and you haven't even met the drill sergeant yet. In fact, the haircut and the uniform may be given to you a couple of hours before you meet the drill sergeant, all to teach the discipline of waiting. They teach the basics of being a soldier—how to make your bed, how to follow directions, because if you can't follow directions in the mundane things, you won't follow directions in a firefight.

There is a heavy emphasis on team-building exercises to teach you how to rely on your fellow soldier. You are paired with a battle buddy (typically your bunkmate). You come to rely on him; you share late night talks together; and you share a bond with him. In the church of God, do we not also need battle buddies? People we bond with, people we encourage, people we pray with, people we help through the twists and turns of the Christian walk?

Fit for Heaven

After seven months, Brian found himself in a war zone. He told me that basic training prepared him, but it didn't really hit him until they were told to "lock and load" while crossing a bridge. He thought to himself, *Wow, I may have to shoot somebody, and somebody might be shooting at me.* He added, "Basic training helped me; I would have freaked out. The armed forces do a great job of making you into a soldier."

And what, Seventh-day Adventist Christian, are you and I being made into? Do we even know? Our key scripture is the Recruitment Brochure: "So roll up your sleeves, put your mind in gear, be totally ready to receive the gift that's coming when Jesus arrives. Don't lazily slip back into those old grooves of evil, doing just what you feel like doing. You didn't know any better then; you do now. As obedient children, let yourselves be pulled into a way of life shaped by God's life, a life energetic and blazing with holiness. God said, 'I am holy; you be holy' " (1 Peter 1:13–16, *The Message*).

Fully devoted

We are being made for holiness, and that means we have a transformation to undergo too. Even as a military boot camp transforms a civilian into a soldier, we need transformation from "civilian" churchgoers into fully devoted disciples of the Lord Jesus Christ. Disciples who are ready for His coming; disciples who are committed to doing the will of God instead of their own will; disciples who won't freak out when the flaming arrows of the evil one start flying; disciples who are fit for heaven. *Boot camp is about being ready for the wedding and serious about the war.*

Let's begin our boot camp with a familiar story. In a way it's a bridal boot camp that proves that weddings are serious business—especially this one:

> "At that time the kingdom of heaven will be like ten virgins who took their lamps and went out to meet the bridegroom. Five of them were foolish and five were wise. The foolish ones took their lamps but did not take any oil with them. The wise ones, however, took oil in jars along with their lamps. The bridegroom was a long time in coming, and they all became drowsy and fell asleep.
>
> "At midnight the cry rang out: 'Here's the bridegroom! Come out to meet him!'
>
> "Then all the virgins woke up and trimmed their lamps. The foolish

ones said to the wise, 'Give us some of your oil; our lamps are going out.'

" 'No,' they replied, 'there may not be enough for both us and you. Instead, go to those who sell oil and buy some for yourselves.'

"But while they were on their way to buy the oil, the bridegroom arrived. The virgins who were ready went in with him to the wedding banquet. And the door was shut.

"Later the others also came. 'Lord, Lord,' they said, 'open the door for us!'

"But he replied, 'Truly I tell you, I don't know you.'

"Therefore keep watch, because you do not know the day or the hour" (Matthew 25:1–13).

The part of the story that is bothersome occurs when the host says, "I don't know you" (verse 12). Why does he say that? It gives us a clue that fitness for heaven has to do with our relationship to God.

We know this is a parable directed to believers because it's about "the kingdom of heaven." So it's about fitness for heaven. Secondly, the protagonists in the story are "virgins." In Bible symbolism, a virgin represents the pure bride of Christ, in contrast to the harlot of Revelation 17, who is dressed in purple and scarlet and is riding on a scarlet beast. She represents an impure church with impure doctrine. These virgins, therefore, represent the bride of Christ, and they are all pure in faith. *False doctrine or error is not the issue. The issue is knowing or not knowing God.* This should give us pause because the implication is that one can possess pure doctrine and still not know God! There was nothing noticeably different about these women. They all wore lovely bridal gowns. They all carried the same lamps, were going to the same party, and had the same invitation. Unfortunately, the bridegroom was delayed, and they all got sleepy and napped. But falling asleep was not the problem.

When the bridegroom finally arrived and the drowsy attendants scrambled to their feet, there was an immediate and distinct difference between the women. That difference was oil. In the Bible, oil is a symbol for the Holy Spirit (Zechariah 4:1–14). The Holy Spirit's job is to lead us into all truth (see John 16:13) and to implant the teachings and principles of Jesus into our lives so that we are remade into His image. "The Holy Spirit produces this kind of fruit in our lives: love, joy, peace, patience, kindness, goodness, faithfulness, gentleness, and self-control" (Galatians 5:22, 23, NLT).

Those with the oil possessed the character of Jesus. Those without the oil

Fit for Heaven

did not, and that is why they were not recognized by the host. Without the Holy Spirit, their characters were unchanged, and their lights couldn't shine.

"Thy word is a lamp unto my feet, and a light unto my path" (Psalm 119:105, KJV). The Word of God is the lamp, but it can be a light only if we live by its principles. The book *Christ's Object Lessons*, describes it this way, "Through the Holy Spirit, God's word is a light as it becomes a transforming power in the life of the receiver."[2]

Without the transforming power of the Holy Spirit, we remain unchanged "civilian" church members, with no light and no spiritual life. Again, *Christ's Object Lessons* says, "One may be familiar with the commands and promises of the Bible; but unless the Spirit of God sets the truth home, the character will not be transformed. Without the enlightenment of the Spirit, men will not be able to distinguish truth from error, and they will fall under the masterful temptations of Satan."[3] Without the principles of the Bible being implanted into our lives, it's accomplishing nothing.

This is why we need to be in God's boot camp for the last days: to have our characters transformed so that we will bring glory to God and not fall for the temptations of Satan. What is the glory of God? Remember when Moses prayed, asking God to show him His glory?[4] God caused His goodness to pass before Moses. As He passed by Moses, He declared, "The LORD, the LORD, the compassionate and gracious God, slow to anger, abounding in love and faithfulness, maintaining love to thousands, and forgiving wickedness, rebellion and sin" (Exodus 34:6, 7). Essentially God said, "OK, Moses, you want to see My glory? I'll tell you who I AM." The glory of God is His character, and "the last message of mercy to be given to the world, is a revelation of His character of love. . . . In their own life and character they [Christ's followers] are to reveal what the grace of God has done for them."[5] The last message to be carried to the world is not a time prophecy or a retreat to the Old Testament ceremonies. The last message for the world is a revelation of God's character *in your life*! Your testimony of His presence in your life—how He has changed and transformed you—is the light of the world!

The oil makes the difference. Without it, it's like a gun without bullets, a flashlight without batteries, a smartphone without cell service, and the form of godliness without the power. We're not ready for the wedding and not serious about the war.

Boot Camp for the Last Days

Dual application

The primary focus of the story is the church's preparedness at the Second Coming. But I wonder whether there was a parallel with the preparedness of Jesus' generation for His first coming. It was almost as if the present experience of the disciples was a preview of what would be happening with the disciples at the end of time.

Luke 17:20–22 describes the experience:

> Once, on being asked by the Pharisees when the kingdom of God would come, Jesus replied, "The coming of the kingdom of God is not something that can be observed, nor will people say, 'Here it is,' or 'There it is,' because the kingdom of God is in your midst."
>
> Then he said to his disciples, "The time is coming when you will long to see one of the days of the Son of Man, but you will not see it."

This is the same attitude Peter describes about scoffers in the last days: "Where is the promise of his coming? for since the fathers fell asleep, all things continue as they were from the beginning of the creation" (2 Peter 3:4, KJV). Three years had passed since John the Baptist announced that the kingdom of God was here. Now the Pharisee skeptics are asking Jesus, "Where is this kingdom You keep talking about?" Jesus tells them it's not what they're looking for. It's within them. It's among them. He was the kingdom of God in the flesh.

In Luke 17:22, Luke records Jesus' words, "The time is coming when you will long to see one of the days of the Son of Man, but you will not see it." They didn't realize what a great privilege they had in having the Living Word of God *with* them. And one day they would kick themselves for not taking greater advantage of the privilege they had. If the Written Word is a light to our path, what kind of light and illumination is the *Living* Word? The disciples had been with Him, but they had not known or appreciated Him. In this sense, we see that Jesus' entire generation "slept" at the time of His first coming. The Pharisees and the disciples were all asleep to who Jesus really was and the nature of His mission.

The coming of the Holy Spirit at Pentecost was the awakening for the disciples. After they had received the baptism of the Spirit (the oil), they finally understood His teachings, His miracles, and the prophecies about Him. It's

Fit for Heaven

no surprise that the Spirit is often described as the sevenfold spirit of God. Isaiah 11:2 calls it

> the Spirit of wisdom and of understanding,
> the Spirit of counsel and of might,
> the Spirit of the knowledge and fear of the Lord.

Everything they lacked before was available to them in buckets now. "They were as men awakened from a dream."[6]

This occurrence parallels Matthew 25:7: "all the virgins woke up and trimmed their lamps." The disciples woke up after they received the oil. At least with the disciples, we could cut them some slack because they hadn't received the gift yet, but what's our excuse? We've had the Gift now for two thousand years. The Holy Spirit is available to us, but we neglect Him. The results of receiving Him are the same: waking up from a dream, understanding who He is and what it means to be saved—to be ready for the wedding and serious about the war.

Looking back on the opportunity that was theirs, the disciples saw "how dimly had they comprehended the prophetic scriptures! how slow they had been" to understand His mission and nature. They were ashamed that "their faith had been so feeble, that their ideas had been so wide of the mark."[7] "What were we thinking?" Is this not sometimes an all-too-accurate description of our spiritual condition today? Do we struggle with dim comprehension, poor understanding, feeble faith, and off-the-mark ideas about the kingdom right now?

Why is this? The disciples were filled with remorse because "they had allowed the prevailing unbelief to leaven their opinions and becloud their understanding."[8] What are we allowing to cloud our understanding? And what of the physical connection? If our bodies (which in 1 Corinthians 6:19, Paul says are "temples of the Holy Spirit") are sick and taxed to their limits due to fatigued organs that are stressed by trying to overcome lack of exercise, poor diets, lack of sleep, and drugs, can our minds—which are already overstimulated—grasp the great truths of Scripture? Is it a shock that we "bonk"[9] on mysteries of the kingdom? It's hard to develop a taste for the Bread of Life when we continually pig out on the mental and physical junk food of our day! Talk about brain freeze! We are groggy, worn out, and sleep deprived.

Boot Camp for the Last Days

Boot camp is about getting a soldier physically and mentally fit for battle. God's boot camp for the last days is about the same thing. And I cooperate by removing whatever obstructs the ability of the Holy Spirit to dwell in me.

We need to be at our clearest, our sharpest, to discern truth from error. To appreciate the truth and the work of God; to take our stand on the front lines of the battle against the principalities and powers and so on; to counteract the prevailing unbelief, dim comprehension, poor understanding, and off-the-mark ideas about the kingdom of God; and to prepare for the coming of the Bridegroom, we're going to boot camp. We're going to do it together. We're going to do what the disciples did: search the prophecies and rehearse the teachings of Christ. But we must have what they had to be successful—the baptism of the Holy Spirit—or we will not comprehend.

The disciples had been with Him but had not known or appreciated Him! Imagine going to church all those years, listening to countless sermons, and not knowing Him or appreciating Him. Years wasted being among believers and yet living in unbelief—without oil. I pray this is not the case for anyone reading this today.

Honest disclosure

I have a confession to make. I am more excited about the concept of boot camp than I am about actually going. The thought of preparing myself to encounter God more deeply is more appealing than actually preparing myself. I find myself a rabid fan of watching the Olympics on TV rather than being an Olympian. Can you relate?

I'm with you on this journey. I want to be genuine, not a pretender. I want Christ to know me when He comes, before the cry goes out, "Behold the bridegroom cometh!" (Matthew 25:6, KJV). Because by then it will be too late.

The wise virgins took extra oil. They allowed the Holy Spirit to do the hard work of changing the heart. We tend to want heaven without the hard work of changing to be fit for heaven. But God shows us in this parable that it's not about gaining heaven without the work. It's about remaking us into His new creation. Let's wake up and trim our lamps together.

BASIC TRAINING

- Pray daily for the baptism of the Holy Spirit.

- Read the parable of the wise and foolish virgins in Matthew 25:1–13. Journal your thoughts on this question: If there was a boot camp for these bridesmaids, what would be included in the basic training, and why? What can you learn from this?

- Cooperate with the Spirit to allow the completion of His work in your life.

---

1. Rod Powers, "How to Survive Military Basic Training," Balance, last modified August 9, 2016, accessed August 16, 2016, https://www.thebalance.com/how-to-survive-military-basic-training-3353989.
2. Ellen G. White, *Christ's Object Lessons* (Hagerstown, MD: Review and Herald®, 2003), 414.
3. Ibid., 408, 411.
4. See Exodus 33:12–23; 34:5–7.
5. White, *Christ's Object Lessons*, 415, 416.
6. Ellen G. White, *The Desire of Ages* (Mountain View, CA: Pacific Press®, 1940), 507.
7. Ibid.
8. Ibid., 508.
9. *Bonk* is an athletic term for being exhausted and quitting.

2

Defensive Dining

So whether you eat or drink or whatever you do,
do it all for the glory of God.

—1 Corinthians 10:31

During a mass baptism ceremony, megachurch pastor Rick Warren had an epiphany regarding the connection between spirituality and health. As he was lowering people into the water, he thought, *Man, we're all fat—and so am I!* This wasn't a very spiritual thought, but it was the truth.

> [Rick Warren's] sermon the following Sunday included a confession—he wanted to lose 90 pounds—and a proposal: Let's all get healthy together. To his surprise, more than half of the 22,000 members of his church pledged to join him on the spot.
>
> Warren then reached out to three experts. . . . Together they built a healthy lifestyle regimen around their five F's: faith, food, fitness, focus, and friends.
>
> A year after starting the plan, Warren's congregation had collectively dropped 250,000 pounds.[1]

Parade magazine asked Warren whether he could draw a line between wellness and spirituality. He responded, "You can't love if you don't have the energy to love. If you go home every night and lie on the couch exhausted because you're not eating right and your blood pressure is too high, well, how can you make a difference? I'm interested in helping my people be well so they can make a difference."[2]

It's good that a famous pastor has made the connection between health and spirituality. I applaud him. The health-spirituality connection has been a pillar in Adventism for years. But here is the irony: while others seem to be embracing this connection, many within our faith community are turning away from it—at a time when we need it most. My epiphany came last August when I received a printout classifying me as obese. Again, not a very spiritual thought, but it got my attention and motivated me to make some changes!

In chapter 1, we determined that *boot camp is getting serious about anything you take seriously.* And in these last days of earth's history, we must be ready for the wedding and get serious about the war.

In the parable of the ten virgins, it is clear that what is needed for that readiness is the baptism of the Holy Spirit. It is the Holy Spirit, represented by the oil, that transforms our characters and keeps us in a relationship with Jesus. And we cooperate by removing whatever obstructs the ability of the Holy Spirit to do His work.

Is excess weight or poor health habits obstructing the Holy Spirit's work in our lives? If we are what we eat, then what are we? Is what we've become helping us to prepare for the wedding and get serious about the war?

Boot camp—Babylonian style

Four people who were absolutely clear on this connection were Daniel and his three friends:

> In the third year of the reign of Jehoiakim king of Judah, Nebuchadnezzar king of Babylon came to Jerusalem and besieged it. And the Lord delivered Jehoiakim king of Judah into his hand, along with some of the articles from the temple of God. These he carried off to the temple of his god in Babylonia and put in the treasure house of his god.
>
> Then the king ordered Ashpenaz, chief of his court officials, to bring into the king's service some of the Israelites from the royal family and the nobility—young men without any physical defect, handsome, showing aptitude for every kind of learning, well informed, quick to understand, and qualified to serve in the king's palace. He was to teach them the language and literature of the Babylonians. The king assigned them a daily amount of food and wine from the king's table. They were to be trained for three years, and after that they were to enter the king's service.
>
> Among those who were chosen were some from Judah: Daniel, Han-

Defensive Dining

aniah, Mishael and Azariah (Daniel 1:1–6).

It is very difficult to keep a kingdom together when one must station troops on foreign soil. There will always be resistance to the foreigners. So Nebuchadnezzar decided to work from the inside out—by targeting the young people. Nebuchadnezzar's foreign policy was a brilliant strategy: *conquest through assimilation and transformation rather than by mere occupation.* He especially targeted members from Israel's royal line and the nobility; young people without any physical defect, handsome, brilliant, well learned, sharp-minded—the best of the best. Nebuchadnezzar knew that if he could take the future leadership and break them, he'd possess the whole nation. Take the best and the brightest of Israel and make them something they're not. It was a brilliant strategy; one that Satan still uses with great success today. He still goes after the best and the brightest among our young. He still takes that which is fresh and trainable—not the old and inflexible who are already set in their ways—to mold into his image.

I recently spent a week taking a class in world religions, learning the cultural aspects and major pillars of faith in Islam, Buddhism, Hinduism, and other faiths, and was reminded that culture runs deep. It's not easily changed. So how would Nebuchadnezzar do it? How would he alter the culture of these Hebrews? How could he get the Israelite worldview out and put the Babylonian worldview in? Let me suggest to you that Nebuchadnezzar had his own form of boot camp.

Remember, that for our US military, "The training programs are scientifically and psychologically designed to tear apart the 'civilian' and build from scratch a proud, physically fit, and dedicated member of the United States Armed Forces."[3] With Ashpenaz as the drill sergeant, Nebuchadnezzar designed a training program scientifically and psychologically crafted to tear apart the "Hebrew" (the noble princes of Yahweh) and build from scratch a proud, physically fit, and dedicated member of the Babylonian high court.

The conversion process, or basic training, was to last three years (verse 5), with these three objectives: (1) change the thinking of these Jews by giving them a Babylonian education; (2) change their loyalty by changing their names; and (3) change their lifestyle by altering their diet. This was the thorough, threefold strategy of getting the Hebrew out and the Babylonian in.

Boot Camp for the Last Days

Resolution

Daniel could see that they were trying to change the structure and fabric of who the Hebrews were. He could see the programming that was about to commence. "But Daniel resolved not to defile himself with the royal food and wine, and he asked the chief official for permission not to defile himself this way" (verse 8). *Defile* means "to soil or stain," and Daniel was not going to soil or stain his character.

Daniel knew he was a sacred vessel and would not allow himself to be defiled. He understood that the connection between your physical health and your spirituality cannot be underestimated. Though he and his friends were being forced to go to Nebuchadnezzar's boot camp now, they had been to Yahweh's boot camp first. The purpose of Nebuchadnezzar's boot camp was to bring God's people *into* Babylon. In God's boot camp for the last days, God's purpose is to bring His people *out* of Babylon.

Daniel knew that he was going to be surrounded by Babylonian culture, politics, lifestyles, and values, and if he was going to stay true to God and His ways, he would need his wits about him. And so do we! Because we, too, live in hostile territory, we are to take care of our body "temples" in such a way that God's Spirit can reign there, and not the spirit of Babylon. Realizing where we live and the times in which we live, we determine to live in such a way that the Holy Spirit can work in and through us.

Daniel understood that the great controversy was being played out in this predicament. He could see beyond the plate to the politics. He could see beyond the wine to the warfare. He could see beyond the delicacies to the deception. It's not just a matter of taste; it's a matter of trust—of loyalty, devotion, and worship. Oh, that we would have eyes to see the battle for our souls fought with the fork!

So Daniel comes up with his own plan. Daniel 1:12–14 says, " 'Please test your servants for ten days: Give us nothing but vegetables to eat and water to drink. Then compare our appearance with that of the young men who eat the royal food, and treat your servants in accordance with what you see.' So he agreed to this and tested them for ten days." The King James Version uses the word *pulse* instead of *vegetables*. Pulse includes vegetables, fruit, and protein from plant sources.

In response to the king's offensive, Daniel employs a "defensive dining" countermove, leaving us an example of how to relate to appetite in hostile

Defensive Dining

territory. The first principle of defensive dining: *don't just eat everything that's put in front of you.*

Proverbs records,

> When you sit to dine with a ruler,
>   note well what is before you,
> and put a knife to your throat
>   if you are given to gluttony [appetite].
> Do not crave his delicacies,
>   for that food is deceptive (Proverbs 23:1–3).

The Hebrew word translated "gluttony" is *nephesh*, which means "soul" or "breathing creature." It also can mean desire, greed, lust, and pleasure. In the context of food, it describes a person who lives to eat. This passage specifically refers to emotional eating—those who seek to satisfy some inner craving or desire through food. Daniel's great ancestor, Solomon, is saying that if you have an emotional desire to satisfy and can please yourself with food more than anything else, put a knife to your throat rather than indulge. Solomon warns that emotional eating is deceptive; it only increases the craving, leaving you less satisfied than before.

Appetite is one of the weird cornerstones of the entire great controversy. The first sin recorded in Scripture deals with appetite—*nephesh*—the emotional desire to please and to elevate oneself. Eve eats the fruit of the forbidden tree. Was she hungry? No. But the serpent had awakened an emotional need within Eve to elevate herself. "I can be like God."

Adam joins her and sin enters the world, not through murder or adultery but through food. *Clearly, if you can't control the appetite, you're in trouble in the great controversy.* Some addictions you can flee from or put out of reach (alcohol, drugs, etc.). But the person enslaved to appetite cannot escape. Why? Because everyone must eat food to survive.

Peter urges his readers, "Beloved, I beg you as sojourners and pilgrims, abstain from fleshly lusts which war against the soul" (1 Peter 2:11, NKJV). Speaking of this passage, Ellen White states, "Many regard this text as a warning against licentiousness only; but it has a broader meaning. It forbids every injurious gratification of appetite or passion. Every perverted appetite becomes a warring lust. Appetite was given us for a good purpose, not to

Boot Camp for the Last Days

become the minister of death by being perverted, and thus degenerating into 'lusts which war against the soul.' "[4]

In human beings, the frontal lobe—the seat of judgment and decision making—makes up 33 percent of the human brain, as opposed to dogs, in which the frontal lobe makes up only 7 percent of the brain. In this area of the brain, dopamine is released when you experience pleasure. This creates a reward pathway in the brain, letting you know that you should repeat this behavior. This response is so powerful and so strong that unless God gets control of the reward pathway in your brain, the enemy can neurochemically hijack you into sinful habits and patterns simply by getting to the frontal lobe of your brain, where you make decisions.

These fleshly lusts would naturally extend to the use of stimulants, narcotics, and alcohol. For many years, Adventists held to the standard of abstinence from alcohol. But today, many in the church have come to regard alcohol consumption as a badge of maturity, like a young person who has just turned twenty-one and is legally old enough to do whatever he or she wants to do. (As if drinking alcohol has become a kind of liberation!) But what is so mature about killing off brain cells? It's not just some church rule that many thumb their noses at. It's the Word of God that says, "Wine is a mocker and beer a brawler" (Proverbs 20:1).

> Who has woe? Who has sorrow?
>   Who has strife? Who has complaints?
>   Who has needless bruises? Who has bloodshot eyes?
> Those who linger over wine,
>   who go to sample bowls of mixed wine.
> Do not gaze at wine when it is red,
>   when it sparkles in the cup,
>   when it goes down smoothly!
> In the end it bites like a snake
>   and poisons like a viper (Proverbs 23:29–32).

This is not some arbitrary rule from a committee—it's the Word of God. But increasingly, more of us seem to think we know more than God.

Why do we abstain from alcohol and strong drink? Because we're in boot camp for the last days! We're in hostile territory, and we need our wits about

Defensive Dining

us to be able to discern truth from error. Because when the mind is fuzzy, everything looks right, everything sounds right, and everything feels right. With the clock ticking down, Satan is putting on a full-court press to do everything possible to hijack our frontal lobes so that we can't see past the plate or the bottle to the battle that's raging all around us! He wants to gain control of this 33 percent of our minds so that we can't tell what's up, what's down, what's right, or what's left.

This thought especially impressed me in view of my recent class on world religions. The New Age thinking is, *I'm not religious, I'm spiritual.* It's code for living according to the New Age, which is an amalgamation and borrows from a variety of religions, especially Eastern religions, and closely resembles Hinduism. The goal is to attain a sense of universal consciousness—a sense of oneness with the divine force in the universe. There is no such thing as right or wrong or sin, only a failure to recognize your personal divinity. Our purpose on this journey through life is to reconnect with that divine essence. If you don't achieve it in this life, just wait for the next one. Reincarnation is the doctrine of the second chance and the third chance and the fourth chance. What does this do to the gospel of Jesus Christ? What does that do to the second coming of Christ? If our minds are confused and fuzzy, if our frontal lobes are compromised because of what we put into our body temples, we will not be able to tell truth from error. The "spiritual" rhetoric will sound appealing, reasonable, and preferable.

Yet, for many of us, our battle is not alcohol consumption but the consumption of edible foodlike substances. Ding Dongs, Twinkies, and Ho Hos are not real food. Test it. Put a piece of bread in your cupboard for a month or two, and do the same with a Twinkie. Bread will mold in a week, but after a year that Twinkie will still be fresh. Even the bacteria and the fungus know there's no nutritional value in the Twinkie. Just because something tastes good doesn't mean it is good. Be careful, you might be sitting at the table of Babylon.

"Don't you know that you yourselves are God's temple [sacred vessels] and that God's Spirit lives in you? If anyone destroys God's temple, God will destroy that person; for God's temple is *sacred*, and *you together are that temple*" (1 Corinthians 3:16, 17; emphasis added). Satan is launching an assault on the temple of the Living God. Junk food, sedentary lifestyles, and much of the digital input we get through screens and devices are mind-altering combinations that keep us physically, emotionally, and spiritually drowsy, sluggish, and exhausted. ("I'll get oil for my lamp tomorrow!") And if we're sick and tired, we'll be too weak to pray. If there's one thing we can't afford, it is to be too sick, too tired, and too fatigued to pray!

Not so with Daniel.

> And at the end of ten days their features appeared better and fatter in flesh than all the young men who ate the portion of the king's delicacies. Thus the steward took away their portion of delicacies and the wine that they were to drink, and gave them vegetables.
>
> As for these four young men, God gave them knowledge and skill in all literature and wisdom; and Daniel had understanding in all visions and dreams.
>
> Now at the end of the days, when the king had said that they should be brought in, the chief of the eunuchs brought them in before Nebuchadnezzar. Then the king interviewed them, and among them all none was found like Daniel, Hananiah, Mishael, and Azariah; therefore they served before the king. And in all matters of wisdom and understanding about which the king examined them, he found them ten times better than all the magicians and astrologers who were in all his realm (Daniel 1:15–20, NKJV).

God appointed Daniel to be the interpreter of dreams and visions to help a pagan king understand the truth about the future and the sovereignty of God. To Daniel was entrusted the knowledge of God. His counterparts could not interpret Nebuchadnezzar's dream. Daniel honored God in his body, and his mind was able to grasp the light of divine wisdom and shine it on Nebuchadnezzar.

We, like Daniel, have been entrusted with prophetic understanding for these times. We are called to be modern Daniels to interpret the apocalyptic dreams and visions of Scripture to help an increasingly pagan society know the truth about the future and the sovereignty of God. But if our minds are confused, will we be able to shine the light for others to find their way, or will we be in the dark with them? Whose boot camp are we in? Can we discern the times? Do we recognize the deception for what it is? Eve was tempted to go beyond the Word of God. "You will be like God" (Genesis 3:5). The spirit of

Defensive Dining

Lucifer is the spirit of Babylon, which is the spirit of the New Age. Revelation 14 and 17 let us know that before Jesus comes, the wine of Babylon will again be offered to intoxicate both the nations and, if possible, the very elect. Will we know it when we see it? That's why we're in God's boot camp. So we can clear our frontal lobes and recognize the signs of the times.

How to practice defensive dining

Resolve to obey God. "*Resolve* is a strong word that means to be devoted to principle and to be committed to a course of action. When Daniel resolved not to defile himself, he was being true to a lifelong determination to do what was right and not to give in to the pressures around him. We, too, are often assaulted by pressures to compromise our standards and live more like the world around us. Merely wanting or preferring God's will and way is not enough to stand against the onslaught of temptation. Like Daniel, we must resolve to obey God."[5]

Decide ahead of time to choose God. It's easier to resist temptation if you have thought through your convictions well before the temptation arrives. Daniel and his friends had already made up their minds to be faithful long before they were faced with the Babylonian diet. You've got to know where you draw the line before the line is staring you in the face.

Stand up for God, even in "little" things. The strong moral convictions of Daniel and his friends made an impact on the Babylonian official. God moved his heart. The light of Heaven shone on Babylon instead of the other way around. How we respond to the big pressures to come will depend on how we deal with the little pressures today.

You are God's sacred vessel with a sacred mission. I challenge you to feast on the Bread of Life and not wash it down with the wine of Babylon. "Whether you eat or drink or whatever you do, do it all for the glory of God" (1 Corinthians 10:31).

BASIC TRAINING

- Resolve to obey God.

- When it comes to your diet, where would you say the enemy is most successful at exploiting your weakness? Standing at your own metaphorical tree of the knowledge of good and evil, what tempts you to say, "I want to be God in this"?

- Compare your answer above with Exodus 20:3 and pray about the implications God reveals to you.

- Decide ahead of time to choose God. What is your "defensive dining" strategy?

- Stand up for God. What will this look like for you in the area of health?

---

1. Margy Rochlin, "Pastor Rick Warren's Life-Changing Message: The Connection Between Getting Healthy and Doing Good," Family, *Parade*, November 30, 2013, accessed August 17, 2016, http://communitytable.parade.com/233614/margyrochlin/pastor-rick-warrens-life-changing-message-on-the-connection-between-getting-healthy-and-doing-good/.

2. Ibid.

3. Powers, "How to Survive Military Basic Training."

4. Ellen G. White, *Christian Temperance and Bible Hygiene* (Silver Spring, MD: Ellen G. White Estate, 2010), 54.

5. *The Handbook of Bible Application*, eds. Neil S. Wilson et al., 2nd ed. (Wheaton, IL: Tyndale House Publishers, 2000), s.v. "Convictions."

3

The Last Message

> Then I saw another angel flying in midair,
> and he had the eternal gospel to proclaim to those who live
> on the earth—to every nation, tribe, language and people.
> —Revelation 14:6

Are you ready for part three of God's boot camp for the last days? First, we talked about the essential requirement of the baptism of the Holy Spirit for character transformation. In chapter 2, our focus was on a commitment to better health so that we can keep our minds clear to avoid Babylon's character transformation.

But our minds need to be clear not only for defense (protection against deception) but also for offense (understanding and proclaiming truth). Winston Churchill said that men occasionally stumble over the truth, but most of them pick themselves up and hurry off as if nothing has happened.

Jesus said, "Thy word is truth" (John 17:17, KJV). He also said, "I am the . . . truth" (John 14:6). What are people stumbling over today? God's Word and God's Son; and most pick themselves up and hurry off as if nothing has happened. But if they stumble over and hurry off from an encounter with the truth, they inevitably will exchange the truth of God for a lie and will worship and serve created things rather than the Creator (see Romans 1:25).

In God's boot camp for the last days, we receive basic training in truth for the last days. Among the greatest and most relevant truths we must understand and not stumble over today are those found in Revelation 14:

> Then I saw another angel flying in the midst of heaven, having the everlasting gospel to preach to those who dwell on the earth—to every nation,

tribe, tongue, and people—saying with a loud voice, "Fear God and give glory to Him, for the hour of His judgment has come; and worship Him who made heaven and earth, the sea and springs of water."

And another angel followed, saying, "Babylon is fallen, is fallen, that great city, because she has made all nations drink of the wine of the wrath of her fornication."

Then a third angel followed them, saying with a loud voice, "If anyone worships the beast and his image, and receives his mark on his forehead or on his hand, he himself shall also drink of the wine of the wrath of God, which is poured out full strength into the cup of His indignation. He shall be tormented with fire and brimstone in the presence of the holy angels and in the presence of the Lamb. And the smoke of their torment ascends forever and ever; and they have no rest day or night, who worship the beast and his image, and whoever receives the mark of his name."

Here is the patience of the saints; here are those who keep the commandments of God and the faith of Jesus (Revelation 14:6–12, NKJV).

For nearly a month, multiple countries engaged in a desperate search for Malaysian Airlines Flight 370 that disappeared March 8, 2014. Government sources say that the sharp turn of the Boeing 777 with 239 souls aboard was a "criminal act" committed by someone on board.[1] I thought to myself, *If only a signal could have gotten through to the aircraft's guidance computers with a message correcting the course of the rogue plane, perhaps those lives could have been saved.*

The three angels of Revelation 14 bear such a message. For more than six millennia, God has engaged in a desperate search for the multiplied billions of souls hijacked on spaceship Earth since the events of Genesis 3. The sharp turn of the human race following the Eden deception was definitely a "criminal act" committed by God's own children. Revelation 14:6–12 represents one last communication from heaven's control tower to correct the course of a rogue planet before it runs out of fuel and crashes.

Three angels, one message—the last message to be given to the earth by the last generation of soldiers to be trained in God's boot camp for the last days. Some call them the *remnant*, or the "rest of her offspring" (Revelation 12:17). What is this last message, and how important is it that we understand this communication while we can still hear the fading "pings" of the Holy Spirit?

The Last Message

This chapter will focus on the first part of the message: "Then I saw another angel flying in midair, and he had the eternal gospel to proclaim to those who live on the earth—to every nation, tribe, language and people. He said in a loud voice, 'Fear God and give him glory, because the hour of his judgment has come. Worship him who made the heavens, the earth, the sea and the springs of water' " (Revelation 14:6, 7).

If you don't remember anything else about Revelation 14, remember this: *the good news of Jesus is the heart and soul of the three angels' messages.* This is unmistakably a gospel message. The last message for the last days starts with the good news that Satan is defeated and Christ has won. The King is coming to deliver us and bring His *shalom* (peace).

Dwight Nelson says that "if you want to tweet the mission and message of the Seventh-day Adventist Church, all you would need to tweet would be: #Jesus&Rev.14:6-12." This is our purpose in being here—*to lift up Jesus and proclaim His everlasting gospel, with an appeal for everyone to return to authentic, biblical worship before the end comes.* Don't miss this: if you preach the three angels' messages without the everlasting gospel, you'll have fear without faith, beasts without blessing, and prophecy without peace.

Breaking it down

Angel means "messenger" (Greek: *aggelos*). The three angels are symbolic of human messengers like you and me who go to the world with the urgent appeal of a coming King. The messenger is pictured as "flying in midair," representing speed and urgency. What's the hurry? The hour of God's judgment has come, and the end is near. There's no time to waste. This lets us know that church isn't just about hearing a message but about being and giving a message. The gospel isn't just for our consumption but for our distribution with all deliberate speed.

Imagine if the disciples had eaten the loaves and fishes blessed by Jesus instead of distributing them to the hungry multitude. They would have gotten bloated, the people would have rioted or turned away in disgust, and Jesus, I'm sure, would have chewed them out. But this happens in too many churches today. We're consuming the miracle food of the gospel ourselves, becoming bloated while the people outside starve to death. And God has every right to be angry. *In God's boot camp for the last days, we are in training to deliver the everlasting gospel with intentionality and urgency.*

Boot Camp for the Last Days

What is the everlasting gospel (Greek: "good message")? The good message about Jesus—His birth, life, death, resurrection, and soon return—is good news for every nation, tribe, kindred, and people. *The last message for the last days is free from prejudice*. Racism has no place in the kingdom of God, period.

One thing that confuses many people (Christians and non-Christians) is how people can read the same Bible and come away with such different ideas. The racial superiority issue serves as an example. Some think that there is nothing in the Bible that speaks against believing in racial superiority. But that's a lie. This first message of the first angel proves to us that the gospel is universal and that *everyone* is equal at the foot of the cross. In the words of Jon Paulien, "God shows a breath-taking lack of prejudice. Multi-culturalism is not just a politically correct fad, it is fundamental in God's attitude toward people in all their infinite variety. God shows no partiality, He cares for all peoples."[2]

I am reminded of a story that can be found on YouTube by searching for "Ee-Taow."[3] The story is about the Mouk people who live in Papua New Guinea. A missionary couple went on their own to share the gospel with the Mouk people after being denied a call by their mission board. After months of learning the language and the habits of the people, the couple began to tell the story of Redemption, beginning with Creation and moving through the stories of the patriarchs and prophets.

The teaching went on two times a day over a period of several months, and each time the village was packed. The sick were carried in on stretchers to hear the message, and one lady gave birth in a hut built especially so she could give birth *and* hear the message.

When they arrived at the story of Jesus, He became their hero; the Mouk people absolutely *loved* Jesus. As they listened to the story of His betrayal, they became indignant, asking, "How could that happen to the One we love?" The people grew distraught as they listened to the tale of the Crucifixion; they couldn't fathom what had happened to this Person they fell in love with.

Then came the story of the Resurrection, but here the missionary circled back to the story of Abraham and Isaac at the altar. The missionary hadn't finished the story immediately, and the people had struggled to understand at the time. While waiting to hear how the end of Abraham's sacrifice transpired, the Mouk leaders decided they knew the solution—God would provide a

The Last Message

substitute. While listening to the conclusion of the story, the people began to exclaim, *"Ee-Taow! Ee-Taow!"* which means "It's true!" "It is good!" The missionary told them that if they accepted Jesus and believed His Word, then their sins would be forgiven. Instantly, celebration erupted; and for more than two and a half hours, the Mouk people celebrated that God truly provided a Lamb *for them.*

I wish we still possessed that same spirit of excitement over Christ's sacrifice. *Never* should we hoard the gospel or grow bored with it. We've been given what this world is looking for. Unfortunately, "the god of this age has blinded the minds of unbelievers, so that they cannot see the light of the gospel that displays the glory of Christ, who is the image of God" (2 Corinthians 4:4). The enemy has blinded the eyes, and taking the blinders off is the purpose of this last message.

The first angel's message is a dual one—fear the Judge and worship the Creator. "He said in a loud voice, 'Fear God and give him glory, because the hour of his judgment has come. Worship him who made the heavens, the earth, the sea and the springs of water' " (Revelation 14:7).

What does it mean to "fear God"? I've boiled it down to three words: Taking God seriously. Why? Because of the everlasting gospel! God took *you* seriously! The Cross is not just some pop psychologist's five-step plan to a better life; it is the power of God for salvation, and it shows how seriously God takes sin and how seriously He loves you and me. Nothing is more serious. So just before He comes back, because of the seriousness of the gospel and the seriousness of the hour, He tells us to take Him seriously. Therefore, the last message of the last days is *take God seriously.*

How?

- *Live with an awareness of God* (Psalm 33:18). To fear God is to know that He is watching us wherever we are, whatever we do. This is not a scary surveilling in order to smite you, but He's watching us with "unfailing love, to deliver [us] from death and keep [us] alive in famine" (verses 18, 19). He's watching us to bless us and to be a part of our lives.

- *Get to know God* (Proverbs 2:1–5). This requires investigation and experimentation. A relationship with God cannot be merely mental or theoretical. God tells us to ask, seek, and knock (see Matthew 7:7); to "test" Him (Malachi 3:10); and to "taste and see that [He] is good" (Psalm 34:8). God invites to us be hands-on with Him. Religious ritual and routine actually keep you at a distance. Go deeper. Get closer.

- *Trust God and distrust yourself* (Proverbs 3:5–7). We do the opposite.

- *Hate evil* (Proverbs 8:13). We tend to celebrate it.

- *Keep God's commandments* (Deuteronomy 6:2; Ecclesiastes 12:13; John 14:15).

- *Love and be loved by God* (Deuteronomy 6:5). This immediately follows the command to fear God and to obey His commandments found in verse 2; here we find the command to love—with all our heart, soul, body, and strength.

"Obedience to the law is the visible sign of our love for God. To live in the sight of God is to live with God. Inversely, because we live with God, we live according to His will. True religion takes God consistently and seriously,"[4] writes Jacques Doukhan. "True religion" is perfectly suited for boot camp, which is getting serious about what you take seriously. To fear God is to take Him seriously.

Then, as if to amplify our understanding, the angel says "fear God and give him glory." Giving God glory is more than singing a song, talking in tongues, or handling snakes. It is acknowledging Him in *all* our ways ("So whether you eat or drink or whatever you do, do it all for the glory of God" [1 Corinthians 10:31]). And it is through loving Him in the way He asked to be loved: "If you love Me, you will keep My commandments" (John 14:15, NASB).

The Hebrew word for "glory" is *kabod,* which contains the idea of weight. Imagine a seesaw on which one side holds God and the other side holds the "stuff" of this life (family, career, finances, hobbies, etc.). Not all of the stuff of life is anti-God, but sometimes, we allow the stuff of life to get so heavy that God gets only the leftovers. When we give God glory, we evaluate God against the "stuff," and we value Him above these other things. We shift our weight to the things of God, seeking Him, putting Him first, reading His

The Last Message

Word, praying, doing His business, and proclaiming the everlasting gospel. We weigh God and His commands against self and the ways of the world, and we weight, or value, God higher. We "weight" on the Lord and give Him glory!

The last message for the last days is a wake-up call to "weight" on the Lord—seek Him first in every aspect of our lives. We give Him everything we've got. "Love the Lord your God with all your heart and with all your soul and with all your strength" (Deuteronomy 6:5). This is not casual Christianity. This is boot-camp Christianity. This is not the New Age version but the Rock of Ages version; not virtual reality but biblical reality. This is how busy, attention deficit disorder (ADD) people living in the twenty-first century, with the most distractions of any generation that's ever lived, keep their minds stayed on God and obtain the oil of the Holy Spirit we talked about in chapter 1. We evaluate life against a relationship with God and throw our "weight" on Him.

When you sit down for a meal, *"fear God and give him glory."* When you select a movie to watch or music to download, *"fear God and give him glory."* When you go on a date or choose a life partner, *"fear God and give him glory."* In your marriage, in your job, in your finances, among your friends, on the Internet, or on the town, in how you dress and adorn your body, in your language and how you treat those who vex you, whatever you do, *"fear God and give him glory"!*

Why? Because the hour of His judgment has come! *Boot camp for the last days is about living all out for Jesus in the judgment hour of Earth's history!*

And judgment is good news! Please see that the proclamation of God's judgment hour is included in the everlasting gospel. In the last days, we must understand both. It is a spiritual abortion to separate the gospel from the judgment, even as it is to separate the law from grace. The two go together.

This is the one thing people of the New Age reject. (Sadly, this includes some Christians; yes, even some Seventh-day Adventist Christians.) They judge that the judgment is negative, and New Agers judge reincarnation as positive because it gives people the opportunity over the course of numerous lifetimes to learn the lessons of love and to perfect their characters. But what sounds positive at first becomes negative when you consider that in the process of learning the lessons of love, we will inevitably do other bad things. And that means we would have to come back again and again to pay for these things (this is karma). The cycle of cause and effect is a never-ending and hopeless struggle.

But God has a better plan. For every cry asking why bad things happen to good people—when the innocent are taken by disease or drunk drivers; when the war hero is gunned down on his own base; for all the victims of genocide, human trafficking, and/or abuse; and on and on—judgment means justice and an end to the madness. Reincarnation just perpetuates the misery. It is as positive and loving as an eternally burning hell. They're both lies! Hear the message of the everlasting gospel today: fear God and give Him glory for the hour of His judgment has come. It means He is bringing a final end to sin and suffering. Injustice is coming to an end. There is liberty and justice for all—for all who fear Him and rejoice in His gospel.

> "Great and marvelous are Your works,
> Lord God Almighty!
> Just and true are Your ways,
> O King of the saints!
> Who shall not fear You, O Lord, and glorify Your name?
> For You alone are holy.
> For all nations shall come and worship before You,
> For Your judgments have been manifested" (Revelation 15:3, 4, NKJV).

Judgment is good news, but only for those who take God seriously and give Him glory. I want to give Him glory today; how about you?

BASIC TRAINING

- Live with an awareness of God. It's hard to be aware of someone you don't communicate with. Out of sight, out of mind. We can't see God, so how do we maintain an awareness of Him? Based on your answer, how aware of God are you?

- Get to know God. How are you doing this? Churchgoing is a start but is not nearly enough. How might a practical approach to Matthew 5–7; 25:31–45; Isaiah 58:6–12 help you?

- Trust God and distrust yourself. How does this work in real life? What does distrusting yourself look like on a daily basis?

- Hate evil. Most people think they do. Define *evil*. Spend some time writing down subtle ways you embrace evil.

- Keep God's commandments. Not in a legalistic way, but how are you allowing God's commandments to "keep" you?

- Love and be loved by God. What does this mean to you? Could you get your answer into a tweet (140 characters)?

---

1. "Sources Call MH370 Turn a 'Criminal Act,' " CNN video, 3:01, March 31, 2014, http://www.cnn.com/videos/world/2014/03/31/tsr-robertson-dnt-malaysia-airliner-criminal-act.cnn.

2. Jon Paulien, "Tuesday, September 02, 2014," *The Battle of Armageddon.com* (Daily Devotional), September 2, 2014, accessed August 18, 2014, http://www.thebattleofarmageddon.com.

3. "Ee-Taow: The Mouk Story," YouTube video, 23:56, posted by "New Tribes Mission," May 13, 2014, accessed August 17, 2016, https://www.youtube.com/watch?v=hjRTBQcf-uc.

4. Jacques B. Doukhan, *Secrets of Revelation* (Hagerstown, MD: Review and Herald®, 2002), 125.

4

Worthy Worship

> "Fear God and give him glory, because the hour of his judgment has come. Worship him who made the heavens, the earth, the sea and the springs of water."
>
> —Revelation 14:7

Welcome to stage four of God's boot camp for the last days. Having first received some basic training in the baptism of the Holy Spirit, then a review of healthy living, we began to reexamine three of the most important communications from heaven to Earth, given just before the return of Christ. They are found in Revelation 14—three angels, one message—the last message to be given to the earth by the last generation of soldiers to be trained in God's boot camp for the last days.

We began with the first part of the message: "Then I saw another angel flying in midair, and he had the eternal gospel to proclaim to those who live on the earth—to every nation, tribe, language and people. He said in a loud voice, 'Fear God and give him glory, because the hour of his judgment has come' " (Revelation 14:6, 7a).

From this we learned that *the good news of Jesus is the heart of the three angels' messages.* The Cross shows how seriously God took us; consequently, our response to so great a salvation is to "fear God" or *"take God seriously."* Get real about your relationship with Him. Live with an awareness of God; trust Him, distrust yourself; hate evil—don't play with it; keep His commandments; and love Him with everything you've got.

When you love God seriously, you give Him glory. You weigh God against everything else—your job, friends, money, tastes, and preferences—and you value Him above them all. *The last message for the last days is a wake-up call to*

Boot Camp for the Last Days

"weight" on the Lord and seek Him first in every aspect of our lives.

Why? Because the hour of His judgment has come! And judgment is *good news*! Jesus will bring a final end to sin and suffering. This war will not go on forever. Unlike most of the wars waged on Earth, with God there is an exit strategy! There will be justice and vindication for the saints of God.

Now let's finish the message of the first angel. Coming on the heels of the command to proclaim a gospel message that takes God seriously is an appeal for worthy worship: "Worship him who made the heavens, the earth, the sea and the springs of water" (Revelation 14:7b). The final message to humankind before the end of time is an urgent call for worthy worship. And *worship that is worthy is centered in the good news of Jesus, fears God, gives Him glory, and honors Him as Creator.*

In the final crisis of the final days, worship matters. It matters *who* we worship, *how* we worship, and *why* we worship.

Who we worship is God. Which God? He "who made the heavens, the earth, the sea and the springs of water." The Creator God. Why does it matter? After all, Hinduism has 330 million gods! New Age religions claim we are all gods. Atheism declares there is no God, and the third angel's message to follow describes a rival power demanding worship as God. So why is it important which God we worship? Because *the first angel's message is clear that the only God worthy of our worship is the Creator God*; and it is designed to prepare human beings to identify the true God and to stand firm against "identity thieves" in the time of crisis.

Proskyneó (pros-koo-neh-o), the Greek word for "worship," means to kiss the master's hand; to crouch towards; prostrate oneself in homage (do reverence to, adore). We see an example in Daniel 3, which tells the story of Nebuchadnezzar's golden image.

Though initially impressed with God's vision, Nebuchadnezzar grew to dislike God's foreknowledge of the future. Because of this, Nebuchadnezzar decided he would build a statue to reflect his own vision of the future. Only his statue would be all gold—boldly stating that there would never be any other king or kingdom to succeed his. So he erected a statue and covered it over with solid gold. (Just because you don't like God's revelation of the future, doesn't mean you can create your own plan or religion. But we do it all the time!)

On a specific day, at a given signal, everyone gathered on the plain of Dura

Worthy Worship

was to bow down in worship to the statue. Daniel refers to "the image" that the king set up nine different times in chapter 3 to impress on the reader that the statue was a man-made effort. The Hebrews were commanded to worship (bow down and do reverence and give adoration to) something other than God. Shadrach, Meshach, and Abednego recognized this as a hoax (breaking the first and second commandments) and said, "We will not serve your gods or worship [bow down to] the image of gold *you have set up*" (verse 18; emphasis added).

Recruits of God's boot camp would not engage in unworthy worship of Babylon's man-made god. *Their conflict in ancient Babylon gives us a prophetic preview of the conflict to come with spiritual Babylon, where another worship mandate to another "image" will be enforced.* The issue of worship in the last days will be over man-made religion versus the worship of the true God—and creatorship is how we know the difference.

> "You are worthy, our Lord and God,
>   to receive glory and honor and power,
> for you created all things,
>   and by your will they were created
>   and have their being" (Revelation 4:11).

Everything that has breath owes that breath to the Creator God. *Worthy worship is tied to God's creatorship.*

If it didn't matter who we worshiped, we could worship anything and everything and call it god. And this is the religion of today. Whatever you call god is god for you. Whatever path you take is right for you. Whatever is your higher power is good for you. If that were true, there would be no need for Revelation 14:8–12. No need to warn about worshiping the beast and his image because all worship is equal. If it's your reality, it's all good. Right?

Wrong. Verses 8–12 say it's not all good. It's unworthy worship because it omits the everlasting gospel, doesn't take God seriously, does not value Him above all else, ignores His judgment (in fact, condemns God's judgment as judgmental), and gives honor and obedience to a power other than the Creator.

Even secular minds acknowledge some sort of a moral standard. For example, a nationwide manhunt began in 2014 for a pastor accused of sexually abusing up to ten young girls for roughly ten years.[1] "Victor Barnard, a pastor at River Road Fellowship in Finlayson, Minnesota, allegedly told his victims that it was God's word for them to have sex with him and that he was 'Christ in the flesh.' "[2]

If all roads lead to heaven and whatever you call God is god in your reality, then what Pastor Barnard did is OK. But even a secularist knows this is *not* OK. All worship is not equal; and if you don't read the Word of God to see what He actually said and did, you may end up worshiping the beast of Babylon instead of the King of kings.

Recently I was discussing this portion of the first angel's message with some young adults in the class I teach every Sabbath morning. I asked them why a call to return to worship of the Creator God was so important. Why would a focus on the creatorship of God be relevant today?

After some long pauses and a not a few blank looks, we probed the implications and it all became clear. The origin of life in the universe is as hotly debated as ever today. Evolution is being peddled as fact, not theory. If evolution is true and God is not the Creator of all life, then Genesis 1 is a myth and there is no God. If Genesis 1 is myth, then so is Genesis 2, and there is no Sabbath, and no divine plan for the sexes or the family. If Genesis 2 is myth, then so is Genesis 3, and there is no such thing as "sin," rendering the first prophetic proclamation of the coming Messiah (Genesis 3:15) irrelevant. And if Genesis 3 is myth and there is no sin, then the Cross means nothing! Jesus was merely a historical figure—another good man who died a tragic martyrs death. The entire Bible would be just another piece of epic literature like the Iliad or the Odyssey.

And this is why a call to worship the Creator is of utmost importance. Acknowledging the Creator and the creation story also acknowledges the entrance of sin and validates the need for a Savior. No Creator = No sin = No Messiah. Unworthy worship ultimately gets rid of Jesus!

And *how we worship is directly linked to whom we worship*. Worship is not paying homage or reverence to ourselves—like kissing a mirror instead of kissing the hand of God. It is just as unworthy to make worship about us and our tastes as it is to worship a false god.

After the fall of man, God instituted the sacrificial system that would represent the coming Redeemer. Blood had to be shed in order to atone for man's sin. The innocent lamb represented the Son of God, who would sacrifice His

Worthy Worship

life on behalf of humanity. The sons of Adam and Eve, Cain and Abel, joined their parents in offering sacrifices for their sins. Abel was a shepherd, and he brought a lamb—his best lamb—to offer as a sacrifice. God accepted Abel's offering. Cain was a farmer—a good farmer—and he couldn't wrap his mind around God's requirement that the sacrifice must be a lamb. Cain may have thought, *Abel's into lambs; I'm into farming. I don't like God's specifications, so I'm going to create my own.*

So instead of a lamb, Cain brought some of the produce from his labor as a farmer. I have no doubt that it was the *best* of Cain's produce. But God rejected Cain's offering. It can't be the best of what *you* can do; it must be the best of what *Jesus* did. Abel's sacrifice honored God. Cain's honored himself. It was a product of his preference and his convenience. God rejected it as unworthy worship.

Cain would probably fit right in to many American churches today because, as one blog states, "Some churches have embraced a business-oriented 'the customer is always right' approach to worship that places individual comfort at the center of Sunday service."[3] Since when did individual comfort become the highest priority in worship? Here's a newsflash: most of what God tells us in His Book is anything but comfortable! In fact, if you're looking for something to make you feel comfortable, you'd better find something else to read! God is not trying to make us comfortable in our sins. His Word makes us uncomfortable with sin so that we will turn from it and bow toward the Savior. *Worthy worship is based on the Word of God, not the comfort of man.* The Bible doesn't just want to speak to us, it wants to detoxify us.

But we're into accommodation today. We keep lowering the bar because of our ever-increasing thirst for gain without pain—for that which costs us nothing.

Once, while watching a discussion on ESPN between *Pardon the Interruption*'s hosts, Michael Wilbon and Tony Kornheiser, my attention was caught as they turned the conversation to golf and the pros and cons of a fifteen-inch cup. The Professional Golfers' Association is trying to find a way to boost participation since golf attendance and play are down. Acknowledging that golf is a difficult, expensive, and lengthy game (four hours to complete), they sought a solution to this dilemma. What did they come up with? Make the hole bigger! As I pondered this solution, it struck me, "That's mini golf!"

Churches around the country are doing the same thing. Because attendance

Boot Camp for the Last Days

is down and denying self and taking up your cross are distasteful to most people, Christianity is in trouble. The solution? Make the goal easier and more enjoyable for the recreational believer—the believer in a hurry who needs his or her worship "to go" with a few free toys inside to make sure you go away happy. It's "selfie" worship.

Selfies are very popular. There are even selfie apps, such as Facetune that can clean up your blemishes and yellowed teeth and smooth your skin texture—all to make sure you look your best. Babylon promotes "selfie" worship—a worship of image over substance. It looks like the real thing, but apps have covered up the imperfections and defects so that it looks and sounds appealing.

Whatever our style of music, prayer, and so on, it must be for the purpose of kissing God and not our preferences, talents, or comfort. Worship is not to be consumed as a product but given in glory to God (valuing Him higher than anything else). Worship that is worthy prostrates self; worship that is unworthy promotes self.

We can't overlook the truth that if the creatorship of God is the basis for worthy worship, then the same is true regarding the signature of the Creator on His creation—which is the Sabbath.

In the final message to the world, it is clear that true worship is contrasted with false (or beast) worship. It is equally clear that worthy worship is connected to the commandments of God (Revelation 14:12). Which commandments? There are a lot of commandments in Scripture. From the language of verse 7, we know we're talking about the Ten Commandments and in particular, the fourth.

Compare "Worship him who made the heavens, the earth, the sea and the springs of water" (Revelation 14:7) to "In six days the Lord made the heavens and the earth, the sea, and all that is in them" (Exodus 20:11). Revelation 14:7 is a parallel passage, an echo of the fourth commandment in Exodus 20. Not only this, but chapters 12–14 of Revelation contain an obvious structural parallel to the commandments of God. (Compare Revelation 12:17 and 14:12 with 13:4, 8 and Exodus 20:3. Also compare Revelation 13:15 with Exodus 20:4–6.)

Consider this statement: "The biblical summons to worship 'Him who made,' the Creator-God, must include a call to return to the keeping of the seventh-day Sabbath. . . . Instituted at Creation, it is embedded in the Ten Commandments written by God's own finger. In an age that presents

Worthy Worship

evolution as the explanation of how life began, there is to be a clear and decisive appeal to return to the understanding of God as Creator and to observe the only day that Scripture identifies as being sanctified and blessed—His memorial of creatorship, the seventh-day Sabbath."[4]

The Sabbath is about much more than what day you go to church; it's about which God you honor as worthy—the God of Creation and salvation, or the god of tradition and convenience. And how we worship today has a lot to say about how we will worship tomorrow in the coming crisis with Babylon.

Recently, Steve, a member of my congregation, shared with me an amazing testimony about God's response to honoring the Sabbath in his life. He was applying for work, and the application process was difficult. He was nervous; and after leaving, he felt defeated and thought that the whole thing was a waste of time.

After settling down a couple of hours later, he decided to move on the next day but was surprised when the company called him and wanted an immediate interview. It is important to note that the trucking industry doesn't take weekends off. So, during the interview for a highly sought-after job, when he mentioned that he wouldn't work on Saturdays, the potential employers were surprised. In fact, their surprise turned to shock when Steve told them he was prepared to walk away from the opportunity if he couldn't have Sabbaths off.

Afterward, Steve described the experience, "I felt blessed to be there. I knew that if God wanted me there, I would be there. I felt confident—the Lord has always provided." He went home, expecting that to be the end of it. But a couple of days later, he received another call, and they eventually offered him the position. As a fellow Christian, his employer has asked further questions about the Sabbath, and Steve has had opportunities to witness to him. Every day God has shown Himself through the open doors He has provided because of Steve's stand for the Sabbath. There will be a time in the future where we all will be faced with a question: will we stand for the Sabbath?

John T. Anderson says this, "When we examine the Scriptures, it becomes clear that *obedience* is the highest form of [worthy] worship, and that without it all worship is meaningless."[5]

Worthy worship is more than group therapy, and the everlasting gospel is more than self-esteem. Worthy worship takes God seriously, takes God's

Word seriously, and takes God's law seriously. In the first angel's message, God lovingly prescribes the remedy for Babylonish identity theft in the last days. In fact, the entire three angels' messages are an outpouring of God's love to His people, saying, "Look, a crisis is coming. Babylon is going to rise again. And out of love for you, I am giving you the remedy for avoiding Babylon's deception and fate: fear God, and give Him glory by keeping the commandments of God and the faith of Jesus."

Worthy is the Lamb!

BASIC TRAINING

- Prepare to worship on Sabbath by worshiping all week.

- Pray with your face to the ground. Not all the time, but experiment to see how a change of position brings about a change of focus.

- Pray when you enter worship space—for others as well as yourself, to connect with God.

- Sing to the Lord.

- Come to church prepared to give, not just to take. How much preference and convenience is wrapped up in your worship experience?

- Bring your Bible (listen for God's instructions for change in your life).

---

1. Catie L'Heureux, "Everything You Need to Know About Victor Barnard, the Creepy Cult Leader Accused of Sexually Assaulting Minors," Crime, *The Cut,* June 21, 2016, accessed August 19, 2016, http://nymag.com/thecut/2016/06/pine-county-minnesota-sex-offender-victor-barnard.html.

2. HLN staff, "Pastor's Alleged Sex Victim 'Robbed of Childhood,' " *Nancy Grace*, HLNtv.com, April 21, 2014, accessed August 22, 2016, http://www.hlntv.com/video/2014/04/21/victor-barnard-pastor-sex-victim-robbed-childhood. Barnard was captured in Brazil in early 2015. David Lohr, "Victor Barnard, Fugitive Minnesota Cult Leader Accused of Child Molestation, Captured in Brazil," *Huffington Post*, March 2, 2015, accessed August 19, 2016, http://www.huffingtonpost.com/2015/03/02/victor-arden-barnard-captured_n_6784086.html.

3. Constance M. Cherry, quoted in John Blake, "Stop Dressing So Tacky for Church," *Belief Blog,* CNN, April 19, 2014, http://religion.blogs.cnn.com/2014/04/19/stop-dressing-so-tacky-for-church/.

4. John T. Anderson, *Three Angels, One Message* (Hagerstown, MD: Review and Herald®, 2013), 21.

5. Ibid., 113 (emphasis added).

5

Don't Drink the Kool-Aid

> " 'Fallen! Fallen is Babylon the Great,'
> which made all the nations drink the maddening
> wine of her adulteries."
> —Revelation 14:8

"Drinking the Kool-Aid" is a figure of speech commonly used in the United States that refers to the wholesale acceptance of a belief, argument, or philosophy without critical examination. We might also say gullible consumption; swallowing something "hook, line, and sinker"; or "taking the bait." It could also refer to knowingly going along with "a doomed or dangerous idea because of peer pressure."[1]

The phrase came from the November 1978 Jonestown Massacre, in which members of the Peoples Temple, who were followers of the Reverend Jim Jones, committed suicide by drinking

> a cocktail of chemicals including cyanide, diazepam (aka Valium—an anti-anxiety medication), promethazine (aka Phenergan—a sedative), chloral hydrate (a sedative/hypnotic sometimes called "knockout drops"), and most interestingly . . . Flavor Aid—a grape-flavored beverage similar to Kool-Aid. . . .
>
> . . . Jones first insisted that mothers squirt poison into the mouths of their children using syringes. As their children died, the mothers were dosed as well, though they were allowed to drink from cups. Temple members wandered out onto the ground, where eventually just over 900 lay dead, including more than 300 children.[2]

Don't Drink the Kool-Aid

"Don't drink the Kool-Aid" is the way we warn about something deadly that looks innocent; like antifreeze for pets—sweet tasting but death inducing. A third of the angels drank Lucifer's Kool-Aid. Eve drank the serpent's Kool-Aid; Lot's wife drank Sodom's Kool-Aid; Sampson drank Delilah's Kool-Aid; Judas, Pilate, the Pharisees, elders, and teachers of the Law all drank Satan's Kool-Aid. And the final book of the Bible warns of a global "Jonestown" where all the nations consume another kind of Kool-Aid.

"A second angel followed and said, ' "Fallen! Fallen is Babylon the Great," which made all the nations drink the maddening wine of her adulteries' " (Revelation 14:8). To the first angel's message, calling every living being to take God seriously and to worship Him worthily, is added a second end-time message warning us not to drink the "maddening wine" of Babylon. Just before Jesus comes again, the whole world will be forced to drink a poisonous cocktail of lies that will make Jonestown pale in comparison. And the same heart of love that gave us the everlasting good news in the first message now says in this message, "Don't drink the Kool-Aid!"

What's in the wine that makes it so dangerous? What or who is Babylon? How are we who are in God's boot camp for the last days supposed to interpret this mysterious message?

There are some readily observable facts about Babylon:

- *Babylon must be symbolic here* because "the great city" was no longer a prominent city by the time John wrote the Apocalypse (A.D. 95). Centuries before, Isaiah wrote,

> Babylon, the jewel of kingdoms,
>   the pride and glory of the Babylonians,
> will be overthrown by God
>   like Sodom and Gomorrah (Isaiah 13:19).

One hundred years later, Jeremiah made a similar prediction (see Jeremiah 50:40). While Isaiah lived, Babylon was destroyed in 689 B.C. by Sennacherib. But it was rebuilt by his son, Esarhaddon. Later, when Nebuchadnezzar became king of Babylon, he made it one of the most beautiful cities of the ancient world. After its capture by the Medes and Persians in 539 B.C., Babylon suffered declining importance as it endured attacks and restorations from Xerxes, Alexander the Great, and Seleucus. Finally, during the reign of Trajan (A.D. 98–117), it was completely destroyed.

- *Babylon must be a superpower* to make all nations drink her Kool-Aid. It exerts a universal power of coercion.

- *Babylon falls or collapses just before the return of Christ* ("fallen, is fallen" [verse 8, KJV]). It is a failed system. Even as the Peoples Temple cult was a failed system ultimately ending in death, the Babylonian superpower is a failed system that ultimately kills those who drink its wine.

Nimrod

Nimrod, a descendant of Noah's son Ham, was the founder of Babylon. "[Nimrod] became a mighty warrior on the earth. He was a mighty hunter before the LORD. . . . The first centers of his kingdom were Babylon, Uruk, Akkad and Kalneh, in Shinar" (Genesis 10:8–10). His name came from the Hebrew verb *marad* ("to rebel"). The Septuagint interprets verse 9 as "a mighty hunter *against* the Lord." In other words, he's the author of imperialism, forming the first confederacy of tribes. He also moved society from a patriarchal society to a monarchical system.

Nimrod was the first to carry on a war against his neighbors, conquering the regions from Assyria to Libya. Under his leadership, the Tower of Babel was attempted. "Come, let us build ourselves a city, with a tower that reaches to the heavens, so that we may make a name for ourselves; otherwise we will be scattered over the face of the whole earth" (Genesis 11:4).

Here we start to see the two great sins of Babylon:

1. *Doubt of God's word*. God promised in Genesis 9:11 that He would not flood the earth again.
2. *Defiance of God's will*. God told Noah and his family in Genesis 9:1–4 to multiply and "fill the earth."

God says, "Go!" Nimrod and his subjects say, "We're staying." God says, "I will not flood the earth." Babylon says, "Why trust what God says, when we are capable of securing our own future and making a name for *ourselves*."

Don't Drink the Kool-Aid

Like kissing a mirror, Nimrod wanted to make his own name glorious, not the Lord's. He echoed Lucifer's words, "I will be like the most High" (Isaiah 14:14, KJV).

As we said previously, *just because you don't like God's vision of the future doesn't mean you get to create your own.* To do so is Babylonian. It is to rebel. It is drinking the Kool-Aid.

Babylon (Bab-ilu) literally means "gate of the gods." The Hebrews associated it with *Balal*, meaning "to confuse." "That is why it was called Babel—because there the Lord confused the language of the whole world. From there the Lord scattered them over the face of the whole earth" (Genesis 11:9). Put together, *Babylon* means the "confusing gate of the gods." Babylon was the gateway for people to access a pantheon of gods—a multitude of gods. Babylon was the Amazon.com of deities. All of the deities were accessible through Babylon. And, ultimately, whoever keeps the gate is in charge.

This flies in the face of Jesus, who said, "I am the gate; whoever enters through me will be saved" (John 10:9). Jesus is not the gate of the "gods," but He is the gate to the One true God. No one comes to the Father but by Him (see John 14:6).

Babylon's claims are opposed to Christ, which makes it antichrist. "All who have come before me are thieves and robbers" (John 10:8). Babylonians confused other people with their lies. Instead of a gateway to the gods, they were in rebellion against God. Babylon implanted malware on the world's computer—duping them into opening a link that exposed them to a virus of spiritual confusion.

Who, then, is behind Babylon? A millennium after Babel, Isaiah crafts a proverb against the king of Babylon. Isaiah records,

> On the day the Lord gives you relief from your suffering and turmoil and from the harsh labor forced on you, you will take up this taunt against the king of Babylon:
>
> How the oppressor has come to an end!
>   How his fury has ended! . . .
>
> All your pomp has been brought down to the grave,
>   along with the noise of your harps;

> maggots are spread out beneath you
> > and worms cover you.
>
> How you have fallen from heaven,
> > morning star, son of the dawn!
> You have been cast down to the earth,
> > you who once laid low the nations!
> You said in your heart,
> > "I will ascend to the heavens;
> I will raise my throne
> > above the stars of God;
> I will sit enthroned on the mount of assembly,
> > on the utmost heights of Mount Zaphon.
> I will ascend above the tops of the clouds;
> > I will make myself like the Most High."
> But you are brought down to the realm of the dead,
> > to the depths of the pit (Isaiah 14:3, 4, 11–15).

Lucifer is the invisible king of Babylon. It is his spirit of pompous defiance and lust for God's throne that drove Nimrod, Nebuchadnezzar, and the Babylon of the Apocalypse. It is a rival institution to the true church of God—those who keep the commandments and have the faith of Jesus.

Babylon has three distinct characteristics:

1. disobedience to God's Word,
2. defiance against God's will,
3. a desire for God's throne.

By the close of the first century A.D., Christians were already connecting Rome with Babylon: "The church in Babylon, also chosen, sends you greetings, as does Mark, my son" (1 Peter 5:13, HCSB). The literal city of Babylon was an uninhabited waste at the time, so this reference is a prophetic look at the fate of spiritual Babylon to come at the end of time.

As imperial Rome gave way to papal Rome, the spirit of Babylon was detected in the medieval church by Reformers like Martin Luther. With the Pontifex Maximus ("great bridge builder") being the bridge to God (gateway

Don't Drink the Kool-Aid

to the gods) and claiming the power on Earth to forgive sins (confession) and the power to change God's times and laws (altering the Ten Commandments and bringing in Sunday worship), Martin Luther nailed his ninety-five protests to the Wittenberg castle door. And later, in 1520, he wrote, "If they [the pope and all the Romanists] do not abrogate all their laws and traditions, restore proper liberty to the churches of Christ, and cause that liberty to be taught, then they are guilty of all the souls that perish in this miserable servitude, and that the papacy is identical with the kingdom of Babylon and the Antichrist itself."[3] Strong words from Luther.

Other Reformers arrived at the same conclusion Luther did: *Babylon is an apocalyptic symbol of all religious bodies and movements that have fallen away from the truth, especially the fallen Roman Church*—the geopolitical power that will rise and fall before the coming of Christ. The system of Roman Catholicism that finds its roots all the way back in Nimrod.

Babylon is a spiritual-political superpower that will lead a universal apostasy among the nations, substituting human laws and expediency for the laws of God, and will appeal to the secular powers of the state to enforce them. This is the "maddening wine," the Kool-Aid that the second angel warns against.

But what's the danger for us? I'm concerned that we are drinking *the Kool-Aid of compromise*. Some of that is a confusing rationalization that we can be like the world and still be like Jesus, that we can play in the dark but still walk in the light. But we're fooling ourselves.

During the time of King Ahab, the Israelites tried to serve the Lord and Baal, failing woefully in the process. At Mount Carmel, while calling the Israelites to a revival of true godliness, Elijah said, "How long will you waver between two opinions? If the Lord is God, follow him; but if Baal is God, follow him" (1 Kings 18:21).

Even as the end gets nearer, we seem to have less and less time for God. For us, the most dangerous Kool-Aid may not be false doctrine but *frozen truth*. Truth that we refrigerate and do nothing with—like the veggie patties I bought from Costco, placed in the refrigerator, and days later went to use on a sandwich. I was shocked and disgusted to discover they had grown hair! Mold, yuck! I had ignored them for too long, and they spoiled. Truth that we don't consume every day, not just in what we believe but in how we live, will spoil. Or rather, we will spoil while the truth remains.

Boot Camp for the Last Days

I'm concerned that we are drinking *the Kool-Aid of ingratitude*—a neglect of opportunities and blessings that leads to spiritual indifference and a lack of love. We're too busy, exhausted, and distracted to pray, read the Word, and serve. "There is a stupor, a paralysis, upon the people of God, which prevents them from understanding the duty of the hour."[4]

Remember the disciples in Gethsemane? Jesus asked them to pray and keep watch for just one hour, but they couldn't stay awake. Even the sight of an angel from heaven could not keep them awake. Now, as we enter the darkest time in Earth's history, Jesus is still asking His followers to pray and keep watch. And once again, an almost supernatural stupor hovers over us, threatening to overwhelm us with sleep, just as the disciples were overwhelmed in Gethsemane. In order to escape the slumber that threatens to overcome, we must avoid drinking the Kool-Aid of sexual immorality—same sex or otherwise; of science; of agnosticism; of external religion that leaves the heart unchanged; of prayerlessness; of perfectionism; and of unforgiveness.

Following His triumphal entry, Jesus wept over Jerusalem. Why? Because He saw the destruction to come from drinking Babylon's wine—the city and people of God getting in bed with and committing adultery with the citadel of Satan. Is Jesus weeping over spiritual Jerusalem today?

When Jesus was on the cross, when the work of our redemption was so close to being finished, He was offered wine to drink, mixed with gall (myrrh), a narcotic designed to numb the senses. But Jesus refused to drink the wine of Rome. He said No to the Kool-Aid; He would drink the Father's cup to the full. For those in God's boot camp for the last days, Jesus is our example. Don't drink the Kool-Aid! Not now. Not when the plan of salvation is so close to being finished. Not when we need our senses about us the most.

How do we stay clear of Babylon's Kool-Aid? *The call to worthy worship of the Creator is given as a protection against the confusion of Babylon.* Out of gratitude for being saved by the everlasting gospel, fear God, give Him glory, worship Him, keep His commandments, and drink deeply of the Water of Life. What are you drinking?

BASIC TRAINING

- Practice worthy worship (Psalm 95:6, 7; Romans 12:1). How might you be consuming Babylon's "wine" (Kool-Aid)? Be honest in this exercise, and pray about what you discover.

- Practice truth (John 8:31, 32; Ephesians 6:14; 2 Timothy 2:15). This is a call to integrity. What is truth? Does it matter? Why, or why not?

- Practice the art of gratitude (Philippians 4:6, 7, 1 Thessalonians 5:16–18). How will you do this on a daily basis? How would gratitude counteract the effects of Babylon's wine?

---

1. *Wikipedia*, s.v. "Drinking the Kool-Aid," last modified August 11, 2016, https://en.wikipedia.org/wiki/Drinking_the_Kool-Aid.

2. Chris Higgins, "The Jonestown Massacre: The Terrifying Origin of 'Drinking the Kool-Aid,' " *Mental Floss*, November 8, 2012, accessed August 19, 2016, http://mentalfloss.com/article/13015/jonestown-massacre-terrifying-origin-drinking-kool-aid.

3. Martin Luther, *On the Babylonian Captivity of the Church*, quoted in James M. Kittelson, *Luther the Reformer: The Story of the Man and His Career* (Minneapolis, MN: Augsburg Fortress Press, 2003), 152.

4. White, *Christ's Object Lessons*, 303.

6

The "March" of the Beast

> This calls for patient endurance on the part of the people of God
> who keep his commands and remain faithful to Jesus.
> —Revelation 14:12

The above scripture comes at the end of the last message to be given to the earth by the last generation of soldiers to be trained in God's boot camp for the last days. Let's begin here before we back up and consider the third and final angel's message.

"This calls for patient endurance on the part of the people of God who keep His commands and remain faithful to Jesus" (Revelation 14:12). What calls for steadfast "endurance" on the part of the saints? What will threaten to push them to the edge of despair if it weren't for their stubborn endurance and refusal to let go of God's commandments and the true and everlasting gospel? The context shows that it is clearly the tremendous struggle with Babylon, the beast, and his image—a battle that began in heaven: "Then war broke out in heaven. Michael and his angels fought against the dragon, and the dragon and his angels fought back" (Revelation 12:7). The battle then came to Earth: "The great dragon was hurled down—that ancient serpent called the devil, or Satan, who leads the whole world astray. He was hurled to the earth, and his angels with him" (verse 9). The serpent targeted Christ: "The dragon stood in front of the woman who was about to give birth, so that he might devour her child the moment it was born. She gave birth to a son, a male child, who 'will rule all the nations with an iron scepter.' And her child was snatched up to God and to his throne" (verses 4b, 5). And then the dragon went after Christ's bride, the church: "Then the dragon was enraged at the woman and went off to wage war against the rest of her offspring—those who keep God's

The "March" of the Beast

commands and hold fast their testimony about Jesus" (verse 17). The war, the rage of the dragon against the church, calls for "patient endurance."

Not long ago, the world held its breath to see whether there would be a war between the United States and Russia over the Ukraine crisis. But that's not the conflict that requires patient endurance on the part of God's people. The spiritual war of the ages, the great controversy between Christ and Satan and its final showdown as described in Revelation 13 and 14, is the conflict that should have our undivided attention.

But I fear it does not. The truth is, while we post and tweet and text and snapchat and game and eat and drink and marry and give in marriage and sleep, *the beast is on the march.*

Even as the disciples slept in Gethsemane, unable to watch and pray with Jesus for one hour, Judas and his mob—an odd confederacy of church and state, religious leaders and Roman soldiers—made their way, under cover of darkness, through the olive trees to arrest God's Son.

The sleepy disciples did not recognize the betrayer among them any better than we recognize the beast among us. You see, *sometimes we get so caught up in deciphering the mark of the beast in the future that we fail to detect the* march *of the beast in the present.*

A while back, something unsettling occurred to me. The proclamation of the most solemn messages given to humankind prior to Christ's return are given during the final dispensation, or era, of the church. What is that final era? The era of Laodicea. Let that sink in. *The most intense message to be given to humans is to be delivered by the church that is neither cold nor hot.* A white-hot message is in the hands of a lukewarm church.

What does that look like? I'd have to say it looks an awful lot like this: People ask, "How are you doing?" We reply, "Fine." You may be lying through your teeth, but "fine" is the acceptable answer so that is what we say. When people ask me, "How is the church?" I say, "Fine. We're OK. We're holding services and collecting offerings. Our attendance is so-so, and our online viewings are up. Prayer meeting attendance is down, but we have monthly potlucks and walks in the park; we bless babies and have occasional baptisms. We're paying down debt and paying our bills—we're here. We're all right."

But is "all right" really all right? Are we to be "fine" or on fire? Laodicea is not just a concept or a theological idea. It's real, and we are the church of Laodicea. We can't pick the era into which we are born any more than we can

Boot Camp for the Last Days

pick which country or family we're born into. We have no say in that. For reasons that God alone knows, we've been chosen to live and minister and be disciples of Christ in *Laodicea*; and this, too, requires patient endurance on our part. Maybe because God wants to show what it looks like for people to wake up and be on fire in a lukewarm environment. There is a lot of talk about climate change in the global environment; but right now, I am praying for a climate change in the church.

What are we to do? The answer comes to the church of Philadelphia:

"Since you have kept my command to endure patiently, I will also keep you from the hour of trial that is going to come on the whole world to test the inhabitants of the earth.

"I am coming soon. Hold on to what you have, so that no one will take your crown" (Revelation 3:10, 11).

That is the key to patient enduring.

Hold on to what you have! I pray to God that what you have is Jesus. Because holding on to a profession of Christ, to a church membership, to a religious philosophy, or to anything else won't cut it. *To patiently endure is to hold on to Jesus and the commandments of God when it is hardest to do so.*

We may think it is hard to hold on right now, but Revelation tells us that it is going to get much worse. We must endure in season and out of season; when we feel like it and when we don't; when it's convenient and when it's inconvenient. Yes, in Laodicea now—the time of "all right" Christianity, spiritual stagnation and sleepiness. In our small groups, in our homes, alone with God's Word and face down on the carpet before Him, we must hold on to the fear of God and His worthy worship now so that we can hold on to those things under the pressure of the beast power tomorrow. Why? Because for a time, Babylon and the beast are going to have the upper hand, and what you believe is going to get you in trouble. This calls for patient, steadfast endurance.

Now we're ready for the final message: "A third angel followed them and said in a loud voice: 'If anyone worships the beast and its image and receives its mark on their forehead or on their hand, they, too, will drink the wine of God's fury, which has been poured full strength into the cup of his wrath' " (Revelation 14:9, 10). This is the most solemn warning of the three messages.

The "March" of the Beast

What or who is this beast, and what is the mark? We can't decipher chapter 14 without chapter 13; the two are linked together:

The dragon stood on the shore of the sea. And I saw a beast coming out of the sea. It had ten horns and seven heads, with ten crowns on its horns, and on each head a blasphemous name. The beast I saw resembled a leopard, but had feet like those of a bear and a mouth like that of a lion. The dragon gave the beast his power and his throne and great authority. One of the heads of the beast seemed to have had a fatal wound, but the fatal wound had been healed. The whole world was filled with wonder and followed the beast. People worshiped the dragon because he had given authority to the beast, and they also worshiped the beast and asked, "Who is like the beast? Who can wage war against it?"

The beast was given a mouth to utter proud words and blasphemies and to exercise its authority for forty-two months. It opened its mouth to blaspheme God, and to slander his name and his dwelling place and those who live in heaven. It was given power to wage war against God's holy people and to conquer them. And it was given authority over every tribe, people, language and nation. All inhabitants of the earth will worship the beast—all whose names have not been written in the Lamb's book of life, the Lamb who was slain from the creation of the world.

Whoever has ears, let them hear.

> "If anyone is to go into captivity,
>   into captivity they will go.
> If anyone is to be killed with the sword,
>   with the sword they will be killed."

This calls for patient endurance and faithfulness on the part of God's people (Revelation 13:1–10).

Who is the beast? There are seven points of identification:

1. *Power and authority from the dragon.* "The dragon gave the beast his power and his throne and great authority" (Revelation 13:2). The dragon is Satan (Revelation 12:9).

Boot Camp for the Last Days

    a. The dragon summons the beast from the sea. In prophecy, the sea refers to people: "The waters you saw, where the prostitute sits, are peoples, multitudes, nations and languages" (Revelation 17:15).

    b. It's a confederate beast, whose body parts are from a leopard (Greece), a bear (Media-Persia), a lion (Babylon), and a ten-horned dragon (pagan Rome).[1]

    c. The ten horns are Germanic tribes who overran the Roman Empire as it was nearing its end. Constantine elevated the Christian religion and the bishop of Rome, and it soon became the religion of the state. As pagan Rome fell, papal Rome rose—a combination of both political and religious power.

2. *Rule for 1,260 years.* With Vigilus taking the papal chair in A.D. 537, the Scripture said he would be "given authority to continue for forty-two months" (Revelation 13:5, NKJV). There are 30 days in a biblical month, and 30 x 42 = 1,260. These are the years of papal supremacy, ending in 1798.

3. *Blasphemy against God.* "It opened its mouth to blaspheme God, and to slander his name and his dwelling place and those who live in heaven" (Revelation 13:6). Jesus was accused of blasphemy. In John 10:33 and Luke 5:21, He was accused of claiming to be God and claiming power to forgive sins. What power on Earth claims both as true of itself?

    a. *"We hold upon this earth the place of God Almighty."*[2]

    b. "Does the Priest truly forgive the sins, or does he only declare that they are remitted? The Priest does really and truly forgive the sin in virtue of the power given to him by Christ."[3]

The two things that Jesus was accused of, called "blasphemy," are claimed by the Catholic Church.

4. *Persecutes the saints.* "It was given power to make war against God's holy

The "March" of the Beast

people and to conquer them" (Revelation 13:7). History tells the story of the hundreds of thousands of people who lost their lives during the Spanish Inquisition, the Saint Bartholomew's Day massacre, and in the countries of Europe.

5. *Received a deadly wound.* "One of the heads of the beast seemed to have had a fatal wound, but the fatal wound had been healed. The whole world was filled with wonder and followed the beast" (Revelation 13:3). The time of papal rule was 42 months, or 1,260 years, which ended in 1798. What happened that year in church history? On February 15, 1798, Napoleon's general Berthier marched into Rome and abolished the papal government, imprisoning the pope in France, where he died in prison.

6. *Deadly wound was healed.* "One of the heads of the beast seemed to have had a fatal wound, but the fatal wound had been healed. The whole world was filled with wonder and followed the beast" (Revelation 13:3). On February 11, 1929, Benito Mussolini signed the Lateran Treaty, which gave the papacy the right to be a sovereign government. The *San Francisco Chronicle* wrote this about the agreement: "The Roman question tonight was a thing of the past and the Vatican was at peace with Italy. . . . In affixing the autographs to the memorable document, *healing the wound* . . . , extreme cordiality was displayed on both sides."[4] Once again, church and state were cooperating together.

7. *Universal admiration and devotion to the beast.* "The whole world was filled with wonder and followed the beast" (Revelation 13:3b). The Roman Catholic Church now has more than one billion adherents, and there are 180 ambassadors to the Vatican.

No other power fulfills these seven points. The Roman Catholic Church had led people into captivity and has been taken into captivity itself. Through the power of the state, it had killed with the sword; and by a civil power, it received a mortal wound. From the reading of God's Word and looking at history, we know *the beast is the papacy*—not Catholics, the papacy.

Boot Camp for the Last Days

America rising

In 1798, the church was injured, and its power broken for a while. But even as this first sea beast was falling (going into captivity; see Revelation 13:10), another beast was rising to come to its aid.

> Then I saw a second beast, coming out of the earth. It had two horns like a lamb, but it spoke like a dragon. It exercised all the authority of the first beast on its behalf, and made the earth and its inhabitants worship the first beast, whose fatal wound had been healed. And it performed great signs, even causing fire to come down from heaven to the earth in full view of the people. Because of the signs it was given power to perform on behalf of the first beast, it deceived the inhabitants of the earth. It ordered them to set up an image in honor of the beast who was wounded by the sword and yet lived. The second beast was given power to give breath to the image of the first beast, so that the image could speak and cause all who refused to worship the image to be killed. It also forced all people, great and small, rich and poor, free and slave, to receive a mark on their right hands or on their foreheads, so that they could not buy or sell unless they had the mark, which is the name of the beast or the number of its name.
>
> This calls for wisdom. Let the person who has insight calculate the number of the beast, for it is the number of a man. That number is 666 (Revelation 13:11–18).

All beasts before this one came out of the sea (masses of people, population centers). This one comes up out of the land, far from the sea of the Old World, in the uncivilized New World.

We're given a clue about the purpose of this earth beast in Revelation 12:14–16: "The woman was given the two wings of a great eagle, so that she might fly to the place prepared for her in the wilderness, where she would be taken care of for a time, times and half a time, out of the serpent's reach. Then from his mouth the serpent spewed water like a river, to overtake the woman and sweep her away with the torrent. But the earth helped the woman by opening its mouth and swallowing the river that the dragon had spewed out of his mouth."

In prophecy, a woman represents a church. And in Revelation 12 the earth beast is a haven for God's people (the church, represented by the woman)

The "March" of the Beast

who flee religious persecution during the 1,260 years.

The second beast has horns like a lamb. It doesn't destroy another beast nation that previously occupied its territory. Neither does it start as a global power, but it gradually comes up and takes the land. It is a young nation—like a lamb, not a mature ram.

The horns have no crowns. This is a nation without a king. The horns are lamblike (Christlike). This is a nation that is founded on Christian principles. It follows Christ's teachings on how government and religion are to coexist: "Give back to Caesar what is Caesar's, and to God what is God's" (Matthew 22:21).

It's time to solve the puzzle. What nation was on the rise in the late-eighteenth century, birthed in the New World as a haven from religious persecution—a fresh, young nation that pioneered a representative form of government instead of a monarchy, founded on the Lamb of God's principles of freedom of worship, and has grown into a global superpower?

> One nation, and only one, meets the specifications of this prophecy; it points unmistakably to the United States of America. . . .
>
> The Lord has done more for the United States than for any other country upon which the sun shines. Here He provided an asylum for His people, where they could worship Him according to the dictates of conscience. Here Christianity has progressed in its purity. The life-giving doctrine of the one Mediator between God and man has been freely taught. God designed that this country should ever remain free for all people to worship Him in accordance with the dictates of conscience.[5]

But something happens to this freedom-loving power that causes all who love this nation to shake their heads in disbelief even as the disciples must have done when Jesus foretold the future of their beloved temple.

Revelation 13:11 states, "It spoke like a dragon." Who is the dragon? Satan (Revelation 12:9). He is the same power behind the sea beast (Revelation 13:2). All the powers speak the same language. It's Babylonian (Luciferian). It is the language of lies, arrogance, pomposity, blasphemy, and replacement. "I will be like the Most High" (Isaiah 14:14, KJV). When God speaks, creation happens. When the dragon speaks, deception happens. "He speaks his native language, for he is . . . the father of lies" (John 8:44).

Boot Camp for the Last Days

It pains all of us who love this nation to grapple with the reality that the future is not repentance but rebellion—not freedom but force. "It exercised all the authority of the first beast on its behalf, and *made* the earth and its inhabitants worship the first beast, whose fatal wound had been healed. . . . It also forced all people, great and small, rich and poor, free and slave, to receive a mark on their right hands or on their foreheads, so that they could not buy or sell unless they had the mark" (Revelation 13:12, 16, 17; emphasis added).

How does the lamb beast speak as a dragon? Through the hallmark of all false religion: force and coercion, the language of Babylon. If the prophecy is true and the interpretation correct, there will come a time when this country breaks down the wall of separation between church and state and becomes a persecuting power that will form an alliance with the sea beast, enforcing its worship on everyone else.

Yes, you read that right. The final conflict between the beast powers of the apocalypse and the bride of Christ is what the first conflict was about—worship.

- "People *worshiped* the dragon because he had given authority to the beast, and they also *worshiped* the beast and asked, 'Who is like the beast? Who can make war against it?' " (verse 4; emphasis added).

- "All inhabitants of the earth will *worship* the beast" (verse 8; emphasis added).

- "It exercised all the authority of the first beast on its behalf, and made the earth and its inhabitants *worship* the first beast, whose fatal wound had been healed" (verse 12; emphasis added).

- "The second beast was given power to give breath to the image of the first beast, so that the image could speak and cause all who refused to *worship* the image to be killed" (verse 15; emphasis added).

As secular as you may think the United States is becoming today—distancing itself from the Word of God—the Bible tells us a time is coming when the tables will be turned and the critical issue will be worship.

Just as God directed His people to symbolically imprint His law on their foreheads and hands, representing total obedience and submission both in thought and actions (Deuteronomy 6:8), this land beast forces all people to do the same, not to God's law, but to that of the sea beast. *The "mark" of the beast is more than a superficial tattoo; it's a sign that the sea beast's law is inscribed deeply in people's minds and manifests itself through their actions.*

This is something that could happen only under the influence of Babylon's wine. There are some things that humans do while drunk they would never do while sober. America, according to Bible prophecy, will enact laws and policies that are directly opposite to the values she has always stood for—the preservation of religious freedom. Such an about-face could never happen under normal, sober conditions. Had this nation continued "defensive dining," refusing to consume whatever worldview was put in front of it, it would never change into something it wasn't (a dragon). But under the influence of Babylon's wine, the unthinkable happens.

Unlikely bedfellows

Here in America, there was a time when Catholics were persecuted. The Virginia "House of Burgesses provided that thereafter no 'popish recusants' were to hold office in the colony and that any priest entering its borders was to leave immediately on being warned by the governor. Catholics were likewise disenfranchised and threatened with other persecution."[6]

Is there any evidence of these two powers—one Protestant and one Catholic—mending fences and working together as one?

- Ronald Reagan and Pope John Paul II overthrowing communism.

- President George H. W. Bush's State of the Union address on January 29, 1991: "It is a big idea: a new world order. . . . Only the United States of America has both the moral standing and the means to back it up."[7]

- John Paul II's homily for the World Day of Peace, New Year's Day 2004: "People are becoming more and more aware of the need for a new international order."[8]

- Thomas P. Melady, US ambassador to the Vatican, 1989–1993: "I believe that the U.S., as the world's only superpower, and the Holy See, as the only worldwide moral-political sovereignty, have significant roles to play in the future. Their actions will impact on the lives of people in all parts of the globe."[9]

- "The Pope was recognised as the overall authority in the Christian world by an Anglican and Roman Catholic commission yesterday which described him as a 'gift to be received by all the Churches.' Disagreement about the extent of the Pope's authority was one of the main causes of the English Reformation in the 16th century. . . . If a new united Church was created it would be the Bishop of Rome who would exercise a universal primacy."[10]

- In 2014, the late episcopal bishop Tony Palmer declared Luther's protest "over" to a gathering of charismatic evangelical pastors and leaders at Kenneth Copeland's Word of Faith Movement convention.[11]

And, of course, Pope Francis came to the United States in September 2015 and was received with honors and fanfare unequaled to other world leaders and heads of state. At the invitation of former House Speaker John Boehner, Francis became the first pontiff ever to address a joint session of Congress.

Where is all this headed? According to Scripture, it's headed to a place none of us want to go—Error: 666.

Six is man's number. It symbolizes the self-sufficiency and pride of the person who does not need God. Remember Nebuchadnezzar's statue in Daniel 3? He built the statue to be sixty cubits high and six cubits wide. This triple repetition of the human number shows the desire to take God's role; the number three being the number of God, who is expressed in Three Persons—Father, Son, and Holy Spirit—and who is three times holy. The number 666 shows that, for every declaration of God's holiness, man declares his supremacy. Man-made religion will use the power of the state to enforce its man-made law in defiance of the law of the Creator God.

This is all still in the future; and though no one has the *mark* of the beast yet, we must be aware of the *march* of the beast going on right now. If worship and your relationship to God are on the back burner of your life now, it will be front and center then. You can worship any old way you want to now,

The "March" of the Beast

but one day you will not have that luxury. This nation, which has protected the rights of all to worship freely (or not) according to their consciences, will dare to do what even God won't do—use force to require unworthy worship to a power other than the Creator God.

The issue then won't be whether to sleep in on Saturday or go to church; it won't be whether we sing with a band or with an organ; it won't be whether we clap or say Amen; and it won't be whether we use the KJV or the NIV. The choice then will be the worthy worship of the Creator God—worship that takes Him seriously, gives Him glory, acknowledges Him as Creator, and honors His commandments, of which the seventh-day Sabbath is His signature on Creation—versus the unworthy worship of the beast power that is backed by Satan and who thinks to change the times and laws of God.

> A third angel followed them and said in a loud voice: "If anyone worships the beast and its image and receives its mark on their forehead or on their hand, they, too, will drink the wine of God's fury, which has been poured full strength into the cup of his wrath. They will be tormented with burning sulfur in the presence of the holy angels and of the Lamb. And the smoke of their torment will rise for ever and ever. There will be no rest day or night for those who worship the beast and its image, or for anyone who receives the mark of its name." This calls for patient endurance on the part of the people of God who keep his commands and remain faithful to Jesus (Revelation 14:9–12).

If you're not prepared to hold on to what you have and patiently endure life as it is right now in Laodicea, then it doesn't matter whether you know the meaning of 666 or who the beast is. *Knowing the mark of the beast is irrelevant if you don't know how to hold on to your faith against the daily march of the beast into your soul.* Hold on to what you have.

We don't have a say about the era into which we were born; we're here now. God is saying to each of us, "Wake up, and hold on to what you have. For a while, it will appear as if you are on the losing side; but hold on, for in just a little while, He who shall come, will come." If you don't have a relationship to hold on to, choose *now*!

BASIC TRAINING

- Has God blessed America? Yes. We sing "God Bless America," but we need to pray that America blesses God. A Christian nation? The Bible identifies only one such thing: "But you are a chosen people, a royal priesthood, a holy nation, God's special possession, that you may declare the praises of him who called you out of darkness into his wonderful light" (1 Peter 2:9). You're it!

- The church, not America, is the only "Christian nation" and the true hope of the world. If you're an American and you love this country, then let your light shine! Not in partisan politics, as if one party or the other is the Messiah. Don't become beastly in your defense of the gospel! Too many are speaking like the dragon while professing to follow the Lamb.

- This calls for patient endurance and faithfulness on the part of the saints. It calls for us to spend time studying God's Word. When we don't study God's Word, we fall prey to the deceptions of the dragon's words—lies! Half-truths accompanied by lying "wonders to deceive, if possible, even the elect" (Matthew 24:24).

---

1. For further study, see Daniel 7.
2. Leo XIII, *Praeclara Gratulationis Publicae, Encyclical Letter*, June 20, 1894, Papal Encyclicals Online, accessed August 22, 2016, http://www.papalencyclicals.net/Leo13/l13praec.htm (emphasis added).
3. Joseph Deharbe, *A Complete Catechism of the Catholic Religion*, eds. James Fox and Thomas McMillan, 6th American ed. (New York: Schwartz, Kirwin & Fauss, 1912), 279.
4. "Mussolini and Gasparri Sign Historic Roman Pact," *San Francisco Chronicle*, February 12, 1912 (emphasis added).
5. Ellen G. White, *Maranatha* (Hagerstown, MD: Review and Herald®, 1999), 193.
6. Ray Allen Billington, *The Protestant Crusade* 1800–1860 (Chicago: Quadrangle Books, 1964), 7.
7. George H. W. Bush, "State of the Union Address," January 29, 1991, transcript and video, 47:50, Miller Center of Public Affairs, University of Virginia, http://millercenter.org/president/bush/speeches/speech-3429.
8. John Paul II, "XXXVII World Day of Peace: Homily of John Paul II," January 1, 2004,

Vatican, accessed August 22, 2016, http://w2.vatican.va/content/john-paul-ii/en/homilies/2004/documents/hf_jp-ii_hom_20040101.html.

9. Thomas P. Melady, *The Ambassador's Story: The United States and the Vatican in World Affairs* (Huntington, IN: Our Sunday Visitor Pub., 1994), 10.

10. Oliver Poole, "Churches Agree That Pope Has Overall Authority," BBC, May 13, 1999, quoted in "Churches Agree That Pope Has Overall Authority," Antipas, last modified November 23, 2014, accessed August 22, 2016, http://www.antipas.org/commentaries/articles/authority_pope.html.

11. Ruth Gledhill, "Christians Mourn Death of Bishop Tony Palmer, Friend of Pope Francis," Church, *Christianity Today*, July 22, 2014, accessed August 22, 2016, http://www.christiantoday.com/article/christians.mourn.death.of.bishop.who.was.friend.of.pope.francis/38973.htm.

7

Endurance Training

> If you possess these qualities in increasing measure, they will keep you from being ineffective and unproductive in your knowledge of our Lord Jesus Christ.
>
> —2 Peter 1:8

For the last several chapters, we've taken time to process through what it means to be ready for Christ's coming and how it affects our everyday lives. We've been in boot camp. Why? Because boot camp is where out-of-the-ordinary training takes place to produce an out-of-the-ordinary result. *Boot camp is getting serious about anything you take seriously.* As Seventh-day Adventist Christians living in these times, we want to take God seriously. We want to know how to diligently seek Him now even as the world is just as diligently trying to ignore Him (or at the least, trying to reshape Him into its image).

We learned that in military boot camp, the training is designed to turn the civilian into a proud, fully devoted soldier. Boot camp is a place of change. The church is also to be a place of change, not a museum but a manufacturing plant where fully devoted disciples are made.

We are being made for holiness, changing into disciples who are ready for His coming. Disciples who are committed to doing the will of God rather than committed to doing their own will. Disciples who don't freak out when the flaming arrows of the evil one start flying. Disciples who are fit for heaven. *Boot camp is about being ready for the wedding and serious about the war.*

As we learned in the previous chapter, "This calls for patient endurance on the part of the people of God who keep his commands and remain faithful to Jesus" (Revelation 14:12). This statement appearing after the three angels' messages shows that what calls for the saints' patient endurance is the

Endurance Training

tremendous struggle with Babylon, the beast, and his image.

Preparation for this epic showdown is why we're in God's boot camp. We also learned that *to patiently endure is to hold on to Jesus and the commandments of God when it is hardest to do so.* We must endure in season and out of season; when we feel like it and when we don't; when it's convenient and when it's inconvenient. We must hold on to the fear of God and His worthy worship now so that we can hold on to those things under the pressure of the beast power tomorrow—a power that is on the march in our lives today.

Now I want to go back to Peter where we started, this time to 2 Peter, for some endurance training—some final instructions in holiness that will help us shed some weight so that we can fit into the wedding garments Christ has purchased for us.

When I read this letter, I can't help but notice the similarities to the times in which we live. Even as we can see the steady march of the beast across society and even into the church, Peter was watching the beginnings of that march in the church he loved. "He wrote to warn them of an internal attack—complacency and heresy. He spoke of holding fast to the nonnegotiable facts of the faith, of growing and maturing in the faith, and of rejecting all who would distort the truth."[1]

Haven't you ever wanted to be like Paul or Peter? I want to have an experience like that. We're going to learn that there's nothing that stops you from having that kind of experience. *The only limitations are the ones you place on yourself.* For those in God's boot camp, the good and the bad news is that *you can have as much of God as you want.*

The good news is that the sky's the limit. If you want to walk with God like Enoch did; if you want a connection with the Father like Jesus had; if you want the full measure of the Holy Spirit in your life, it's yours!

The bad news is that the ground, not the sky, is typically what we're content with. God gives us diamonds, and we're happy to play marbles with them. Our crime in not failure but low aim.

In chapter 1, Peter lays out some basic training exercises for those who want a faith that endures to the end. He writes, "His divine power has given us everything we need for a godly life through our knowledge of him who called us by his own glory and goodness" (2 Peter 1:3). This is the divine sandwich. "His divine power" is the first slice of bread. "His own glory and goodness" is the other slice, and in between is "everything we need" for practical life and godliness. *Everything you need to be ready for the wedding and successful in the war, you already have in Christ!* You lack nothing to live the life of Jesus except the will to use what you've been freely given. To a certain extent, whether we have a faith that endures is up to us. We're not just pawns on a cosmic chessboard with no control of our circumstances. God has given us free will—the most powerful gift He could give humans—to use however we want. It's what makes us most like Him.God has done and is doing His part. He is both the Author and Finisher of our faith, but what we do with it is up to us.

"Through these he has given us his very great and precious promises, so that through them you may *participate* in the divine nature, having *escaped* the corruption in the world caused by evil desires" (2 Peter 1:4; emphasis added). To escape my fallen nature, God allows me to participate in His divine nature. How? Through His great and precious promises. His promises are His Word. His Word is His character. When I live by His promises, I'm living "in" His character; and His character knows no corruption, so neither will I. We become "one flesh" with Christ through the promises of God. This is how we become like Jesus! As one of the early church fathers said, "He became what we are to make us what He is."[2]

In God's boot camp, we're not just saved from *something; we're saved* to something—*we're saved to the very nature of God.* How awesome is this?

I love listening to Francis Chan's podcasts. In one of his sermons, I heard him say that if we're looking back at the Bible characters and wishing we could do what they did, something is wrong in our understanding of the Holy Spirit. If we're looking at Elijah on Mount Carmel calling down fire from heaven or at Joshua commanding the sun to stand still or at Paul raising the dead and saying to ourselves, "I wish I could experience God like they did," our spiritual envy is misplaced. Because those we are wishing to emulate were looking to the future, wishing they could be like us!

Go back to the valley of dry bones in Ezekiel 37. Those bones represented Israel's spiritual condition at the time. They were "very dry" (verse 2). Devastatingly lifeless. No hope. Then, while Ezekiel watches, God's Spirit moves over the bones, flesh covers them, breath enters the once-dead bodies, and they stand to their feet, a might army for God.

Through this miracle, God was saying to Ezekiel and to the people of Israel, "There is coming a day and time when I'm going to do this for My people. I'm going to put My Spirit *inside* a human body. It's not going to be

Endurance Training

the Shekinah glory inside the Holy of Holies in the temple anymore. My Spirit is going to be inside human flesh. I'm going to take out the stony heart and put in a heart of flesh. I'm going to write My laws on their minds and hearts, and they're going to love to obey My law (Ezekiel 36:26, 27; Hebrews 10:16). From their heart, they will love Me, and I will make My home in them" (John 14:23).

The people back then who received that message must have been astonished. *"No way! You mean God is going to put His Spirit inside sinful human beings? They're going to have the Spirit of God living inside of them? They're going to be partakers of the divine nature? Shut up!"*

So here they were, looking forward to our day when the people of God would be the dwelling place for the I AM. If we're jealous of the exploits of the Bible heroes, we've got it backwards. Ezekiel was shown the miracle of the dry bones so that he could understand God's plans for Israel and for us. And the way people would freak out if they witnessed those bones coming together and coming to life is the same way people should react to you coming to spiritual life: "What happened to you? I know the way you used to be."

But God put His breath in you and gave you a new heart—a heart that loves His commandments. If you've been born again, that's what He did to you. Your "dry bones" live! We don't realize what we have been saved *to*. We've settled for so little when God has given us so much. We are saved to be partakers of the divine nature.

"For this very reason," Peter writes, "make every effort" (2 Peter 1:5a). What reason? Participation in the divine nature and escaping the corruption of our sinful natures. This, too, requires patient endurance on the part of God's people, who are in His boot camp learning how to obey His commandments and who remain faithful to Jesus. What follows next from Peter is his endurance-training regimen.

"Make every effort" (verse 5). Yes, there is something for Christians to do. In the first five verses of the chapter, Peter has basically said that "everything you need has been given to you by God. In the fifth verse he says, 'Now, give all diligence (intense effort) to add to your faith.' "[3] *Faith makes all things possible, not easy.* Who said this was going to be easy? Jesus didn't promise smooth sailing, only a safe arrival. As long as we're in the Father's will, we'll be all right. Grace has provided a way of escape, but we've got to take it. Our part is to climb the ladder to safety.

Boot Camp for the Last Days

Antoine Turner was a homeless football player coming to play for Boise State University. Antoine was homeless through a variety of unfortunate circumstances, including the death of his mother and Hurricane Katrina. He lost his home and uncle in that disaster. Antoine started over in California, playing football for Fullerton College (a community college), and hoped to graduate in May 2014. But many nights he would sleep on a park bench. News cameras captured Turner at night simply putting his head down between his massive arms as he sat at the park picnic tables.

Turner was expected to move to Boise, Idaho, upon graduation, where a full-ride scholarship awaited him at Boise State. According to the university, Turner would receive "full tuition, room and board, books, fees, etc."[4] Though normal circumstances prohibit colleges from helping athletes, Boise State appealed to the NCAA to be able to help this young man. The NCAA approved the exemption, and a full-ride scholarship was provided. He had everything he needed to succeed, but the university wouldn't open one book, lift one set of weights, or make one tackle. Turner had to do those things. He had to add to Boise State's opportunity his own determination and initiative to make the most of what he'd been given.

The blood of Jesus has purchased a full-ride scholarship to heaven. The tuition has been paid, we have free room and board in the Father's house, and our school uniform has been fitted and paid for. That's what God could do, and we couldn't do that part; but what we can do, we must. We have everything we need to succeed, but we must maximize this amazing opportunity. If grace is so amazing, we've got to do something amazing with it—not to earn salvation but in gratitude for it.

"Add to your faith" (2 Peter 1:5). *Endurance training begins with faith*: faith is the foundation of the Christian life. "Without faith it is impossible to please God" (Hebrews 11:6). *Faith is the blessed assurance that Jesus is mine!*

On that foundation, Peter says, "add . . . goodness" (2 Peter 1:5). This goodness includes virtue and moral excellence. The morals of this world and the morals of Jesus are moving in two different directions. Be sure you are moving with Jesus. You just can't do what everybody else is doing—sleeping with whomever you want, drinking whatever, smoking whatever, or whatever.

God calls us to whatever things are true, noble, right, pure, lovely, admirable, excellent, and praiseworthy (see Philippians 4:8). It requires courage to live this way, and "courage" is the other meaning of endurance. Think Daniel

Endurance Training

in the lions' den or his three friends in the fiery furnace. They'd rather die than dishonor God. That's what it means to be soldiers in God's army, trained to add virtue to their faith.

"To goodness, knowledge" (2 Peter 1:5b). This knowledge is not a mere intellectual knowledge, but a practical understanding of God's ways and plans for your life. "Do your best to present yourself to God as one approved" (2 Timothy 2:15). Do you want to know Jesus and His great and precious promises to learn what you are truly entitled to as a child of God? You've got to know "what would Jesus do" in the situations you face every day. There's only one way to obtain this knowledge—sit at His feet, and learn of Him.

"To knowledge, self-control" (2 Peter 1:6a). *Self-control* is "the ability to take a grip of oneself." Basically Peter is saying, "Get a grip!" Close the gap between what you know and what you do. It doesn't just happen. It takes *every effort* to turn away from that Web site, that Krispy Kreme pastry, or that sexual relationship. Yes, something supernatural and miraculous has happened to us, but it doesn't mean that God doesn't involve us in the process. We are colaborers with God. We do this together.

But don't get it wrong. These are not works of salvation but works of faith. But *we do work*. Faith works. It has a goal to reach. *In God's boot camp, the only way to self-control is God-control.* The only person who can control self is the person under the control of the Holy Spirit.

Some passions never leave you. The alcoholic who remains sober, the addict who remains clean, the compulsive eater who maintains the goal weight—the urges still remain. Just because we get wet in the baptistry doesn't mean these passions get washed away. It's not that the passions are gone, it's that the passions are under the control of the Holy Spirit. They're there, but I choose to live by another power. And that power enables me to keep those passions under control so that they do not have the mastery over me. Jesus is my Master.

"To self-control, perseverance" (2 Peter 1:6b). This is the ability to stand your ground and wait joyfully for God's deliverance. Hebrews records,

> Remember those earlier days after you had received the light, when you endured in a great conflict full of suffering. Sometimes you were publicly exposed to insult and persecution; at other times you stood side by side with those who were so treated. You suffered along with those in prison

Boot Camp for the Last Days

and joyfully accepted the confiscation of your property, because you knew that you yourselves had better and lasting possessions. So do not throw away your confidence; it will be richly rewarded.

You need to persevere so that when you have done the will of God, you will receive what he has promised. For,

> "In just a little while,
>   he who is coming will come
>   and will not delay."

And,

> "But my righteous one will live by faith.
>   And I take no pleasure
>   in the one who shrinks back."

But we do not belong to those who shrink back and are destroyed, but to those who have faith and are saved (Hebrews 10:32–39).

Talk about endurance training! We all feel like quitting. Peter says, "When the trials come, don't quit." The promise is "he who endures to the end will be saved" (Matthew 24:13, NKJV).

"To perseverance, godliness" (2 Peter 1:6c). Become a worthy worshiper of the Almighty God. This, too, requires patient endurance because of all the noise in our world. Look at all the things that compete with our worship! You must learn to live in an atmosphere of worship at all times, even outside of church.

"To godliness, mutual affection" (2 Peter 1:7a). Mutual affection (kindness) is love of the brethren. We are to encourage one another and pray for one another. None of us makes it to the kingdom alone. We make it together. Peter learned this at the Last Supper (John 13). We must serve each other.

"To mutual affection, love" (2 Peter 1:7b). *Agape*, unconditional love, is not a casual love; it is the love that God has shown to us, and it is the end goal of God's boot camp. That's what it is to be a disciple. That's what it is to be a Christian. And God's army is always to be progressing. There is no stagnation in God's army. "For if you possess these qualities in increasing measure, they

Endurance Training

will keep you from being ineffective and unproductive in your knowledge of our Lord Jesus Christ" (verse 8).

Behind Peter's endurance training is a stoic concept called *prokope* or "moral progress." It's the advance of an army towards its objective. Christianity is not just a moment in the pool and then a life of stagnation on the pew. We're going somewhere. We're advancing toward something. What? *The divine nature and the kingdom of heaven.*

Are we an army that never advances? That only does drills but never engages in action? Please, God, no! This is one of God's precious promises to you that you will not live an ineffective life.

> But whoever does not have them is nearsighted and blind, forgetting that they have been cleansed from their past sins.
>
> Therefore, my brothers and sisters, make every effort to confirm your calling and election. For if you do these things, you will never stumble, and you will receive a rich welcome into the eternal kingdom of our Lord and Savior Jesus Christ (verses 9–11).

For those in God's boot camp who have received everything we need for life and godliness, don't waste His grace. It's too amazing!

BASIC TRAINING

- Which of these endurance training activities do you need the most help with?

    - Build faith.

    - Practice moral excellence.

    - Increase knowledge.

    - Exercise God-control.

    - Always persevere.

    - Pursue consecration.

    - Demonstrate kindness.

    - Love unconditionally.

- Do you believe that you have received everything you need for life and godliness? How would it change your Christian experience if you did (or didn't)?

---

1. Introduction to 2 Peter, in *Life Application Study Bible*, New International Version (Wheaton, IL: Tyndale House; Grand Rapids, MI: Zondervan, 2012).
2. Irenaeus, *Against Heresies* 3.19.6, quoted in William Barclay, *The Apostles' Creed* (Louisville: Westminster John Knox, 2005), 64.
3. Jerry Vines, "Spiritual Additives," SermonSearch, accessed August 23, 2016, http://www.sermonsearch.com/sermon-outlines/10100/spiritual-additives/.
4. Andrew Lopez, "NCAA Grants Boise State Waiver Request to Help Homeless Recruit, New Orleans Native," *New Orleans Times-Picayune*, May 14, 2014, accessed August 23, 2016, http://www.nola.com/recruiting/index.ssf/2014/05/ncaa_grants_boise_state_grants.html.

8

Jesus Rising

> He who testifies to these things says,
> "Yes, I am coming soon."
> Amen. Come, Lord Jesus.
>
> —Revelation 22:20

I have to give credit to my son-in-law. His proposal to my daughter Candi was creative, romantic, and a lot of fun. It started with a clandestine rendezvous in a church parking lot. Jesse pulled his car up next to mine. The driver's side window lowered, revealing my daughter's sunglass-wearing boyfriend.

Playing my role to the hilt, I asked, "You got the stuff?" He nodded and handed me an envelope. In that envelope were instructions for Candi—clues for a scavenger hunt that would take her all over the Treasure Valley in Idaho for a prize she knew nothing about.

Everybody was in on the surprise except Candi. She didn't even know Jesse was in town. She was nursing a grudge toward him because he hadn't been able to come to see her on her birthday from his home in Bishop, California. She thought he was in Bishop and that the scavenger hunt was his attempt at making it up to her.

Each stop revealed another clue and retraced places they had gone on dates. Candi was enjoying the game but still had no idea what was coming at the end. Finally, with my wife, Suzette; our second daughter, Crystal; and me looking on from our hidden vantage point, Candi pulled into the Pacific Press parking lot where I worked. It was a Sunday, so the parking lot was empty except for a large charter bus. Her instructions were to get on the bus and call Jesse. We watched as she boarded the bus and moved to the back. She made the call, thinking Jesse was talking to her from Bishop, but his voice

Boot Camp for the Last Days

sounded close, *too close*. Suddenly, Jesse emerged from the bus lavatory; and while she was still trying to recover from the shock and excitement of seeing him in the flesh, he gave her the scavenger hunt prize—an engagement ring and a proposal.

The bus driver had our video camera and was filming the whole thing so that we could see the joyful moment. It didn't work out so well, though, because the driver was crying so hard she couldn't keep the camera still.

They exited the bus to a romantic picnic on the same lawn they would get married on seven weeks later! It was a day to remember for all of us. But however fun the scavenger hunt was, the prize was Jesse. The goal was not the engagement, and it certainly wasn't the scavenger hunt. It was to be together as husband and wife. And literally they couldn't wait to make that happen.

When it comes to Jesus' second coming, prophecy and end-time events can be like a scavenger hunt. Jesus left us clues and signs that His coming was near. But sometimes we get so caught up in the horns and beasts and dates and disasters that we forget *who* we're waiting for. It's almost like the actual appearing of Christ takes a back seat to the *signs* of His appearing. Talking and speculating about last-day events seems to be more interesting than the One coming for us on the last day.

As we prepare to end our boot camp, I want this to be our main takeaway: *don't get so fascinated with the apocalyptic scavenger hunt that you lose sight of the object of the hunt—Jesus Himself.*

Do we see the apocalypse rising? No question. But in all the noise, where's Jesus? It's like trying to find Waldo. There's so much going on that apocalyptic ADD is inevitable. Yet, at the end of the day, if Jesus isn't rising in my life, if He isn't my heart's desire and obsession, I may miss the main purpose of prophecy—to prepare me to be with the One I love.

If you miss this main purpose of prophecy, you face the greatest danger of missing Jesus altogether. It's happened before to some of the best Bible students on Earth, the Jews. An encounter between Jesus and the Jews following a miraculous healing at the pool of Bethesda reveals how it's possible to miss Jesus while studying the Bible.

The day Jesus healed the paralyzed man was the Sabbath. The Jews were incensed and wanted to kill Jesus for Sabbath-breaking and claiming God as His Father. Jesus had a ready defense:

Jesus Rising

"If I testify about myself, my testimony is not true. There is another who testifies in my favor, and I know that his testimony about me is true.

"You have sent to John and he has testified to the truth. Not that I accept human testimony; but I mention it that you may be saved. John was a lamp that burned and gave light, and you chose for a time to enjoy his light" (John 5:31–35).

The Jews missed Jesus because they never took John (a prophet) seriously. They chose to enjoy his light for a time. It was fun to watch the desert wild man preach and baptize. It was a pleasant distraction as long as he said the things they liked, but they abandoned him whenever he became awkward. When the prophet's light got too hot, they retreated to the darkness. Therefore, they missed John's testimony of Jesus.

We must avoid this danger. *For Jesus to rise, stay in the light.* Even if that light exposes your sins, stay with Jesus. Take Him and His prophets seriously. "For the time will come when people will not put up with sound doctrine. Instead, to suit their own desires, they will gather around them a great number of teachers to say what their itching ears want to hear. They will turn their ears away from the truth and turn aside to myths" (2 Timothy 4:3, 4).

Hearing God's Word is never to be another form of entertainment. It's not a game. And it's not only for seasons of apocalyptic excitement. When the hoopla is over, make sure you are still walking with Jesus. Believe His prophets.

"You study the Scriptures diligently because you think that in them you have eternal life. These are the very Scriptures that testify about me" (John 5:39). The Jews missed Jesus because they studied the word, but the Word didn't dwell in them (verse 38). "To the Jew the scriptures were all in all. 'He who has acquired the words of the law has acquired eternal life.' "[1] Yet, the best Bible students in the world rejected Jesus. How does that happen?

1. They read to support their positions, not to find God.
2. They failed to realize that it's all about Jesus. From front to back, the Scriptures testify about Jesus. If we study the prophecies, beasts, numbers, symbols, and signs and refuse to come to Jesus to receive new life, we, like the Jews, will be deceived into thinking we have eternal life when all we really have is virtual life—a form of godliness. *For Jesus to*

rise, come to Him for life. Study the Bible to have a relationship with Jesus, not to win an argument. If Bible study doesn't lead you to a personal relationship with Jesus, it is worthless.

"I do not accept glory from human beings, but I know you. I know that you do not have the love of God in your hearts" (John 5:41, 42).

The Jews didn't really love God; they loved their own ideas about Him. It is possible to diligently search the Scriptures and not have the love of God in your heart. "If I have the gift of prophecy and can fathom all mysteries and all knowledge, and if I have a faith that can move mountains, but do not have love [for Jesus], I am nothing" (1 Corinthians 13:2).

It is possible to be a keen student of prophecy and understand all mysteries and still gain nothing if the love of God isn't in you. That kind of knowledge is worthless. "Knowledge [alone] makes [people self-righteously] arrogant, but love [that unselfishly seeks the best for others] builds up and encourages others to grow [in wisdom]. If anyone imagines that he knows and understands anything [of divine matters, without love], he has not yet known as he ought to know. But if anyone loves God [with awe-filled reverence, obedience and gratitude], he is known by Him [as His very own and is greatly loved]" (1 Corinthians 8:1–3, AMP). *For Jesus to rise, love God with reverence, obedience, and gratitude.*

The Jews missed Jesus because they substituted the praise of men for the praise of God.

> "This nation approaches [Me only] with their words,
> And honors Me [only] with their lip service,
> But they remove their hearts far from Me,
> And their reverence for Me is a tradition that is learned by rote
> [without any regard for its meaning]" (Isaiah 29:13, AMP).

When we compare ourselves with each other and say, "I'm as good as ____," we have fallen into substitutionary worship, which becomes lip service, tradition, and ritual without meaningful worship of the heart. "No, a person is a Jew who is one inwardly; and circumcision is circumcision of the heart, by the Spirit, not by the written code. Such a person's praise is not from other people, but from God" (Romans 2:29). The praise that comes from God is

Jesus Rising

for the one who is circumcised in the heart by the Spirit.

For Jesus to rise, allow the Holy Spirit to "circumcise" (mark) your heart. He marks your heart by cutting away selfishness and implanting Christ's character—the fruit of the Spirit. God must have your heart, or the rituals and traditions mean nothing. As you learned at the beginning of God's boot camp, there is no substitute for the work of the Holy Spirit in your life.

From the beginning, humans have had an obsession with idols—with substituting false gods for the true God. The nation of Israel was lost because of this. Even after the Assyrian exile, they couldn't break the addiction: "Even while these people were worshiping the Lord, they were serving their idols. To this day their children and grandchildren continue to do as their ancestors did" (2 Kings 17:41).

Substitution is the spirit of antichrist, which is the spirit of Babylon. We substitute the serpent's word for God's word, a sacrifice of fruit instead of the sacrifice of a lamb. We look to the Tower of Babel in place of God's rainbow promise, Hagar instead of Sarah, the golden calf instead of the tablets of stone. We hunger for the flesh pots of Egypt instead of the milk and honey of Canaan. We seek Baal instead of Jehovah, the worship of created things rather than the Creator, the commandments of men instead of the commandments of God. We cry for Barabbas instead of Jesus, tradition instead of "Thus saith the Lord." We are distracted and straying instead of watching and praying.

As the apocalypse rises, we must not let the spirit of antichrist rise in our hearts—the sin of substitution. The "gods" of sexual sin, materialism, selfishness, politics, entertainment, greed, envy, arrogance, depravity, hatred, faithlessness, and false religion must not rise above Jesus Christ and His righteousness. Now is the time to let Jesus rise and shine!

The most important question Jesus asks of those waiting for His coming isn't whether the third temple will be built in Jerusalem. It isn't whether Pope Francis will impose a Sunday law. Nor is it whether the antichrist will be a Muslim or whether an asteroid will strike on the last blood moon and end the world. No, the most important question Jesus asks us is the same question He asked Peter: Do you love Me? Do I have your heart? (see John 21:15).

Want to be ready for the wedding?

Let Jesus rise. He must increase; you must decrease.

Let Jesus rise, and if He is "lifted up," He will "draw all people" to Himself (John 12:32).

Boot Camp for the Last Days

Let Jesus rise, "repent and be baptized, every one of you, in the name of Jesus Christ for the forgiveness of your sins. And you will receive the gift of the Holy Spirit" (Acts 2:38).

Let Jesus rise, and "confess with your mouth, '[He] is Lord,' and believe in your heart that God raised him from the dead, [and] you will be saved" (Romans 10:9).

Let Jesus rise, and "do not conform to the pattern of this world, but be transformed by the renewing of your mind" (Romans 12:2).

Let Jesus rise, and "get rid of all bitterness, rage and anger, brawling and slander, along with every form of malice. Be kind and compassionate to one another, forgiving each other, just as in Christ God forgave you" (Ephesians 4:31, 32).

Let Jesus rise, and "everyone will know that you are [His] disciples, if you love one another" (John 13:35).

Let Jesus rise, and "do not be anxious about anything, but in every situation, by prayer and petition, with thanksgiving, present your requests to God. And the peace of God, which transcends all understanding, will guard your hearts and your minds in Christ Jesus" (Philippians 4:6, 7).

Let Jesus rise, and "forgetting what is behind and straining toward what is ahead, . . . press on toward the goal to win the prize for which God has called [you] heavenward in Christ Jesus" (Philippians 3:13b, 14).

Let Jesus rise, and don't "become weary in doing good, for at the proper time we will reap a harvest if we do not give up" (Galatians 6:9).

Let Jesus rise, and

do not throw away your confidence; it will be richly rewarded.
You need to persevere so that when you have done the will of God, you will receive what he has promised. For,

"In just a little while,
he who is coming will come
and will not delay" (Hebrews 10:35–37).

Let Jesus rise, and "we who are still alive and are left will [rise] up together with them in the clouds to meet the Lord in the air. And so we will be with the Lord forever. Therefore encourage one another with these words" (1 Thessalonians 4:17, 18).

Jesus Rising

Let Jesus rise, and don't get so fascinated with the apocalyptic scavenger hunt that you lose sight of the fact that your "Bridegroom cometh" (Matthew 25:6, KJV)!

This, then, is the purpose of prophecy: to declare that there is a God in heaven who is in control of world events, to assure us that Jesus wins, to urge us to live by every word that proceeds from His mouth so that we're not deceived by the lying words proceeding from the dragon's mouth, to prepare us to stand with those who obey God's commandments and remain faithful to Jesus, and to prepare us to be with the One we love—to be ready for the wedding!

Let the blood moons and the asteroids, the popes and the supreme courts, the politicians and the stock markets, and the whatever do their things. *As for me and my house, we will let Jesus rise!*

"He who testifies to these things says, 'Yes, I am coming soon.' Amen. Come, Lord Jesus" (Revelation 22:20).

BASIC TRAINING

- How are you letting Jesus rise in your life? Is something other than Jesus on the rise in your life?

- Have you ever been guilty of getting more fascinated with the apocalyptic scavenger hunt than with Christ Himself? Explain. How can you avoid this trap?

- How did the best Bible students in the world ultimately reject Jesus? Does this happen today? Has it happened to you? In what ways?

- The most important question Jesus asks us is, Do you love Me? Do I have your heart? Do you agree or disagree that this is the most important question? Explain. Write your response to this question.

---

1. William Barclay, "The Witness of God (John 5:37-43)," *William Barclay's Daily Study Bible*, StudyLight.org, accessed August 23, 2016, http://www.studylight.org/commentaries/dsb/john-5.html.

Epilogue

Now!

> Now faith is confidence in what we hope for
> and assurance about what we do not see.
> —Hebrews 11:1

When recruits pass basic training, there's often a graduation, and graduations always feature commencement speeches. I know because I've given my fair share of them. Commencement speeches can be funny, serious, inspirational, or instructive. A good one will do all of the above. We've come to the end of this book; but until Jesus returns, we will remain in His boot camp. Nevertheless, I want to leave you with a commencement message. And that message is one word: *now*!

Matthew records three times when Jesus rebuked His disciples with the words "O, ye of little faith" (KJV): Matthew 6:30, worry about the basics of life; Matthew 8:26, fear in a crisis; and Matthew 16:8, spiritual misunderstanding. Was Jesus commenting on the amount of faith they had or on how poorly they were making use of the faith they had? It can't be the amount because it only takes a mustard-seed amount to move mountains. And, as Peter says, we have "everything we need for a godly life" (2 Peter 1:3). So it has to be that they were using their faith so little.

Francis Chan tells a children's story titled "The Big Red Tractor and the Little Village."[1] Everyone in the village loved the big red tractor. In the spring, they would fire up the tractor; Farmer Dave would sit on it; and everyone would cheer. Then they would gather around and push the tractor and tie ropes on it and pull it. Some days they pulled it ten feet, sometimes twenty feet.

They would do this for months and finish just in time for the rains to

Boot Camp for the Last Days

come, and they would plant. When the harvest came, they would have just enough for the winter to feed the entire village.

One day when Farmer Dave was cleaning the attic, he found the owner's manual for the tractor; and he discovered that if the big red tractor was working correctly, the tractor could plow the field in one day. He told the villagers about it the next day, and they laughed at him. "There's no way in the world the tractor can move by itself." They had pushed and pulled and tugged for generations. Farmer Dave was disappointed, but he was determined. So for several nights, he worked on the tractor, and one day he got it running on its own.

One night he plowed the field that had previously taken three months to plow. The villagers said, "It's a miracle!" or "No; aliens must have come down." But a little boy pointed to Farmer Dave, who was tired and was asleep on the tractor. They had plenty of food that winter; and eventually, they sent food around the world—all because Farmer Dave read the instruction manual.

In the first part of the story, Jesus could have said, "O ye of little tractor." Actually, the tractor wasn't little. It was mighty, capable of doing a lot more than all the people could think or imagine. But they were getting little use out of it. They weren't tapping into its full potential.

I've been feeling a lot like that lately. I feel like we've been pulling or pushing the tractor when God has so much more planned for us. We're like the people who laughed at the farmer; we're slow of heart to believe.

On Sunday evening, after Christ's resurrection, two dejected disciples walked to their home in Emmaus. Unbeknown to them, Jesus joined them and began conversing with them. Jesus observed their discouragement, and they inquired, "How do you not know what has happened?" Before giving them a Bible study on Old Testament prophecy, Jesus said to them, "O foolish ones, and *slow of heart to believe* in all that the prophets have spoken!" (Luke 24:25, NKJV; emphasis added). What was the foolishness of His two traveling companions? *They were slow of heart to believe.*

You see, just as exercising our faith is more important than the amount of our faith, so speed is more important than size. When it comes to faith, it's not how much but how fast! *True faith doesn't wait to believe. True faith trusts right now.* And true faith trusts God until the answer comes.

The two disciples who were traveling to Emmaus were slow of heart to believe because of their disappointment over Christ's death. When we focus

Now!

on our circumstances and disappointments, we lose sight of God's promises, and the response time of our faith becomes slow. Our problem is often not a lack of faith but a slow faith—a slow response time.

Oswald Chambers states,

> The statement in John 7:39—". . . for the Holy Spirit was not yet given, because Jesus was not yet glorified"—does not pertain to us. The Holy Spirit has been given; the Lord is glorified—our waiting is not dependent on the providence of God, but on our own spiritual fitness.
>
> The Holy Spirit's influence and power were at work before Pentecost, but He was not here. Once our Lord was glorified in His ascension, the Holy Spirit came into the world, and He has been here ever since. *We have to receive the revealed truth that He is here.* . . .
>
> It is not the baptism of the Holy Spirit that changes people, but the power of the ascended Christ coming into their lives through the Holy Spirit. . . . The baptism of the Holy Spirit is not an experience apart from Jesus Christ—it is the evidence of the ascended Christ.
>
> *The baptism of the Holy Spirit does not make you think of time or eternity—it is one amazing glorious* now.[2]

So I asked myself, *What are we waiting for?* For the latter rain? Really? Why give us more when we haven't used what we have already been given? We're continually focused on the latter rain instead of on the reign of Christ in our lives right now. If Jesus is not reigning in your life today, you can forget about any kind of rain in the church tomorrow. I've got to stop waiting for a miracle and start living as a miracle. Everything we need we've already been given. No one receives the outpouring of the latter rain who has not already received the early rain—the outpouring of the Holy Spirit at Pentecost. If you don't receive that in its fullness, you can forget about anything else coming. We haven't made use of what we've already been given.

Remember the story of Peter's escape from prison in Acts 12? In an effort to gain the approval of the religious leaders, Herod had arrested and killed James, the brother of John; next he arrested Peter. While awaiting his official death sentence, "Peter was kept in prison, but the church was earnestly praying to God for him" (Acts 12:5).

At the same time, God performed a miracle. At first, Peter thought he was having a vision; but when he realized he was truly free, he made his way to the place where the church was gathered. When Peter knocked on the door, a servant girl, Rhoda, inquired who was there and was so blown away that she ran to tell the church without opening the door. " 'You're out of your mind,' they told her" (verse 15).

They were praying for a miracle that had already happened; and when it manifested itself, they denied it and kept on praying for what had already been granted! They were denying the present miracle in favor of the future miracle. They were hoping for tomorrow and missing the blessing of today. They were focused on *then* instead of rejoicing *now*! And God is showing me that we are doing the same thing.

What are we waiting for? "Now faith is the substance of things hoped for, the evidence of things not seen" (Hebrews 11:1, KJV; emphasis added). *Now* faith is what we need.

Things that slow our faith

I recently texted a prayer partner: "I'm so tired of accepting the mental truth—the ideology of this stuff—without walking on the water *now*! Truth is I'm a coward. I curse the safety of the boat I cling to for fear of stepping out. But after a while seasickness gets old."

I cling to the side of the boat that is bobbing up and down in the storm—sick and afraid to let go, but even more scared to walk to Jesus on the waves. Fear makes us slow to believe and slow to experience what it's like to surf without a board.

Our greatest fear is failure—that we will try and make fools of ourselves when we sink. If we're thinking about and being afraid of failure, it proves we still don't get it. Just like the disciples forgot Jesus was in the boat with them, we also have lost sight of who is with us. We have lost sight of the fact that the risen Jesus—the One who defeated death—is with us. There is no failure in Jesus, and He's with me!

The morning I wrote this I read the following: "Jesus says that God will recognize our prayers. What a challenge! By the Resurrection and Ascension power of Jesus, by the sent-down Holy Ghost, we can be lifted into such a relationship with the Father that we are at one with the perfect sovereign will of God by our free choice even as Jesus was."[3]

Because of what Jesus has already done, I can choose to be one with the

Now!

Father so that when I pray it is as if Jesus is praying. Do I dare think like this? Am I crazy enough to seek it *now*? To believe it *now*? To possess it *now*?

Jesus prayed that we would experience oneness with the Father. "That all of them may be one, Father, just as you are in me and I am in you" (John 17:21). Incredible! Is this a concept to dissect and memorize and theorize in a Sabbath School class but not to actually realize? Who do we think we are?

Friends, that's the problem. We have no idea who we are—in Christ! We are stopped and limited and earthbound by who we are in the flesh, by what is seen instead of by what is unseen. We are controlled by the temporary and only fantasize about the eternal. This is backwards. We are to be controlled by the eternal (unseen) and not sweat the temporary.

"So we don't look at the troubles we can see now; rather, we fix our gaze on things that cannot be seen. For the things we see now will soon be gone, but the things we cannot see will last forever" (2 Corinthians 4:18, NLT).

I see myself—my failures and fickleness—and I lose heart. I lower the bar of what I can become and who I am based on what I see (which is temporary). When I focus on Jesus and His promises and prayer for me (which I can't see with my eyes, only with my faith), I see His victory, His absolute integrity, and His oneness with the Father, and I raise the bar of who I am based on what He's done and what He is (which is eternal).

What am I doing thinking about failure?

I can walk on water *now*!

I can do all things through Christ who strengthens me *now*!

I can be one with the Father even as Jesus and the Father are one *now*!

I can approach the throne of grace with boldness *now*!

I am crucified with Christ, nevertheless I live *now*!

I am the salt of the earth and the light of the world *now*!

I am seated in heavenly places with Christ *now*!

I am complete in Christ *now*!

All of these are *right now* promises for *right now* faith!

Doubt

Doubt debilitates our responsiveness. Those who think too much end up believing too late. Faith is not just about the believing. Faith is more importantly *about the timing*! Slow faith ends up being too little because it's too late!

When the Israelites got to Canaan, the time to believe and enter was *now*,

Boot Camp for the Last Days

not later. You snooze; you lose. They had their moment of opportunity.

The Israelites had the visible signs of God's leading in the pillar of cloud by day and the pillar of fire by night. But as my friend Jim Moon once said to me, "Worship ceases to be worship when you don't move with God. It then becomes narcissistic insubordination." You're worshiping yourself, your comfort, your own thoughts and ideas. The cloud has moved on, but you have remained where you were.

While Jesus arose and ascended to the right hand of God, the priests were still offering lambs in the temple even though the Shekinah was no longer there! They were worshiping at an empty altar. They were still looking forward to the sacrifice already made; the grace already given; the salvation already accomplished. "Yet to all who did receive him, to those who believed in his name, he gave the right to become children of God" *now* (John 1:12)!

A timely faith is far more valuable than an amazing faith. And there is no better time to believe than *now*! Some of you have heard the call to be baptized or rebaptized, and you've let the cloud move on without you. As Paul says, "Behold, now is the accepted time; behold, now is the day of salvation" (2 Corinthians 6:2, NKJV). Don't wait for great faith; use the faith that you have *now*!

When God gave Moses that shepherd's rod, Moses had everything he needed to free the slaves and bring the mightiest army on Earth to its knees. When God gave David the stone for his sling, he had everything he needed to bring down Israel's greatest and mightiest enemy. It wasn't the rod, and it wasn't the rock that provided the victory. These were mere tools in the hands of mere mortals. Any old rod would have worked. Any old stone would do. It was faith in the God who gave the tools that brought the victory.

We don't need the biggest church, the best band, the latest cutting-edge technology, or the hottest evangelism strategy. *All we need is all we have, and all we have is all we need. Because all we need is God; and in Him, we have everything.*

A family lost their thirteen-year-old daughter in a skiing accident; in their grief, they decided to donate her heart. The recipient of Taylor's heart was Patricia, a mother of two boys in Arizona. Over the years, she had grown weaker and weaker, unable to be an active mother and nurse any longer. The organizations who provide organ donations try to keep the recipients and donors anonymous; but in this case, Patricia in Arizona found and contacted

Now!

Taylor's mom. For a while, they corresponded via e-mail and then eventually made arrangements to meet. Taylor's mom desired to hear her daughter's heart beating again.

When they met, the two women embraced and wept for about a minute and then Taylor's dad joined the hug. When they finally finished and tears were flowing, Taylor's mom said, "I know we should probably sit down and talk, but I've got to hear her heart." Patricia produced a stethoscope and put it to her chest. Taylor's mom broke down crying again, but she was so happy, "It's so strong." It was bittersweet. Patricia said, "I'm so sorry and I thank you at the same time."[4]

Taylor's mom wanted to know, "What is the recipient doing with my daughter's heart?" And I think about God asking us, "What are you doing with My Spirit? What are you doing with the Spirit that I gave you? What did you do with the gift of My Son's shed blood? Can I hear the beat of My Son's heart in your chest? What are you doing with His resurrection power? What are you doing with the knowledge that He is sitting enthroned in heaven? What have you done with that?"

My greatest fear is that I'll waste it, that all I will have to show is spasmodic church attendance, a few bucks in the offering plate, devotions (if I have time), and singing a few songs. Is that it? Our answer to God on the day of judgment depends on how we answer the question "what did you do with My grace?" right now.

In Matthew 25:14–30, Jesus told the parable of the talents: a wealthy man gave one servant five talents, another two talents, and a third one talent. On the day of accounting, the first servant brought in his five talents with five additional talents he had earned. The second servant brought in four talents, again doubling the balance. But the third servant brought in his one talent. "I buried it. It's right here, exactly the way you gave it to me. I didn't do anything to improve it. It is intact and pristine—just the way it was when you gave it to me." And the man said, "You wicked, lazy servant!" (verse 26).

The Holy Spirit has been given to us; the presence of the living, resurrected Christ dwells in us now. Don't bury Him. He doesn't want His Spirit back the way He gave Him to us. What have you done with the Spirit that He gave you?

Our answer to God on that day depends on how we answer it *right now*.

BASIC TRAINING

- Trust *now*!

- Believe *now*!

- Act *now*!

---

1. "The Big Red Tractor, by Francis Chan," YouTube video, 3:47, posted by "David C Cook," June 4, 2010, https://www.youtube.com/watch?v=mite667rJnA.

2. Oswald Chambers, "The Life to Know Him," in *My Utmost for His Highest*, ed. James Reimann, updated ed. (Grand Rapids, MI: Discovery House, 1992), devotional for May 27, 2016, accessed August 23, 2016, http://utmost.org/the-life-to-know-him/ (emphasis added).

3. Oswald Chambers, "Undisturbed Relationship," in *My Utmost for His Highest* (New York: Dodd, Mead & Co., 1935), devotional for May 29, 2016, accessed August 23, 2016, https://utmost.org/classic/undisturbed-relationship-classic/.

4. "One Family's Special Gift: An Organ Donation," ABC video, 5:08, September 23, 2010, http://abcnews.go.com/GMA/video/familys-special-gift-organ-donation-11706949.